Beowulf

THE OLDEST ENGLISH EPIC

Translated into Alliterative Verse with a Critical Introduction

by CHARLES W. KENNEDY

OXFORD UNIVERSITY PRESS

Oxford London New York

OXFORD UNIVERSITY PRESS
Oxford   London   Glasgow
New York   Toronto   Melbourne   Wellington
Nairobi   Dar es Salaam   Cape Town
Kuala Lumpur   Singapore   Jakarta   Hong Kong   Tokyo
Delhi   Bombay   Calcutta   Madras   Karachi

printing, last digit 20

Library of Congress Cataloging in Publication Data

Beowulf. *English*.
  Beowulf, the oldest English epic.

  "A selected bibliography": p.
  I.   Kennedy, Charles William, 1882-1969, tr.
PR1583.K4   829'.3   40-11376
ISBN-13 978-0-19-502435-7

Printed in the United States of America

To Elizabeth

CONTENTS

⮫§INTRODUCTION

⮫§TRANSLATION

CONTENTS

FOREWORD

THE present volume offers a translation in alliterative verse, based upon Klaeber's text, of the Old English *Beowulf,* with a brief critical introduction reviewing the more important literary and cultural problems which the poem presents. The *Beowulf* has long been a challenge to the translator, and the renderings of it, both in prose and verse, have been many. Each translation, in its turn, has sprung from the same roots: admiration of the spirited excellence of this oldest of English epics, and desire that its worth may be more widely known to the student and to the general reader who find themselves cut off from the original by difficulties of language.

But the putting of an old and excellent wine into new bottles is a tantalizing task, and rarely completely successful. Even under the gentlest and most skillful handling, something of the bouquet vanishes, and, if the hand is unskillful, the wine itself is spilled. In offering a new rendering of the *Beowulf* I can claim only love of the old poem, and patience in a delicate task.

It has been my endeavor to translate the poem faithfully into authentic modern verse, and to avoid if possible that lack of spontaneity of spirit and flow of narrative that is a besetting snare of the translator. I have employed the four-beat alliterative measure, but without any attempt at strict adherence to the conventional types of Old English half-line. I have not treated any stressed syllable in the line as necessarily alliterative, but have used alliteration, both of vowel and consonant, flexibly and freely both within the line itself and, if it seemed desirable, as a device for binding lines together. In translating the lays that are scattered through the poem, the Sigemund lay, the Finnsburg lay, the Queen Thryth episode, and the Battle of Ravenswood, I have used a longer line to differentiate material of lay from material of narrative, and to indicate by this differentiation the nature of the lays as allusive insertions in the narrative frame. In the case of the Ingeld episode, however, the material is so closely interwoven in a long speech of Beowulf, and made so definitely a part of that speech, that, in this instance, it seemed unwise to attempt such distinctive treatment.

I wish to express my grateful thanks to colleagues who have aided me during the course of this work: to Professors Gordon H. Gerould and Henry Savage, of Princeton, for helpful advice at many points; to Professor Albert Elsasser, of Princeton, for his assistance in the difficult task of selecting from the long array of *Beowulf* scholarship a brief bibliography, and for his helpful interest in this translation from its beginning; to Professor W. W. Lawrence, of Columbia, who read the translation in manuscript, and whose stimulating and suggestive criticisms are reflected in many passages.

Princeton, N. J.   C.W.K.
March 25, 1940

INTRODUCTION

THE Old English *Beowulf* holds a unique place as the oldest epic narrative in any modern European tongue. Of unknown authorship, and dating in all probability from the early eighth century, the poem gives brilliant presentment of the spirit and embodiment of the heroic tradition. Illuminating studies of the *Beowulf*, in comparatively recent years, by Ker, Lawrence, Chambers, Klaeber, Malone, and others, have brought increasing appraisal of the extent to which Scandinavian backgrounds are reflected in its material, literary tradition in its structure, and Christian influence in its spirit.

Of the circumstances under which the *Beowulf* was composed we actually know little, though it is possible to trace with some degree of clearness the evolution of the material from which the poem is shaped. Portions of this material must have originally circulated by oral transmission. The poem itself may well have been developed from an earlier series of epic lays, though no one of these lays has survived. In any case, as Ker has pointed out, the *Beowulf*, in the form in which it has come down to us, is a single, unified poem. It is, he writes,[1] 'an extant book, whatever the history of its composition may have been; the book of the adventures of Beowulf, written out fair by two scribes in the tenth century; an epic poem, with a prologue at the beginning and a judgment pronounced on the life of the hero at the end; a single book, considered as such by its transcribers, and making a claim to be so considered.'

1. W.P.Ker, *Epic and Romance*, p.158.

In the light which modern critical scholarship has focussed upon the *Beowulf*, it has come to be recognized that we have here a poem of cultivated craftsmanship, sophisticated rather than primitive in form, and definitely influenced by literary and religious tradition. The influence of the Christian faith is marked and pervasive. There are evidences, also, which seem to support opinion that the author of the *Beowulf* was familiar with the works of Virgil, and that the structure and development of the poem were influenced by epic tradition as illustrated in the *Aeneid*.[2]

The material of which the narrative is shaped is, in large measure, the material not of primitive English, but of primitive Scandinavian life. In the weaving of the narrative the warp is, in part at least, fashioned from the stuff of Continental chronicle and legend. Names of early Swedish kings, repeatedly mentioned in the *Beowulf*, have correspondence to names of kings listed in the ninth-century *Ynglinga tal*. Names and incidents in the poem relating to the ruling house of the Danes have their analogues in the *Skjoldungasaga*, and in the *Gesta Danorum* of Saxo Grammaticus. The disastrous expedition against the Franks of 516, in which Beowulf's uncle, Hygelac, was slain, is set forth in the *Historia Francorum* of Gregory of Tours, who wrote within seventy years of the events described, and in the eighth-century *Liber Historiae Francorum*.

Into this background are woven dark legends of savage feuds of the Continental tribes, feuds of the Danes and Frisians, the Danes and Heathobards, the Geats and Swedes. At Beowulf's death, the prophecy of Swedish dominion over the Geats derives its tragic foreboding from chanted memories of the bitter tribal battle at Ravenswood. The songs of

2. See pp.lv-lxi.

the minstrel in Hrothgar's hall were fashioned from ancient Continental lays: the dragon-fight of Sigemund, the Volsung; the disastrous battle of Danes and Frisians at Finnsburg.

In a setting shaped of these elements the poet has developed a narrative, the material of which is derived from Continental folk-tale. The haunting of Hrothgar's hall by the night-prowling monster, Grendel, and the troll-wife, his mother; the adventurous journey of Beowulf, the Geat, to Dane-land, and his triumph over the monsters; these central themes in the narrative have their analogues in various versions of the European folk-tale of 'The Bear's Son.' Certain Scandinavian tales of the thirteenth and fourteenth centuries, the *Grettissaga,* the *Samsonssaga,* the *Hrolfssaga,* and others, include elements which show resemblance to this basic material of the *Beowulf,* and the resemblance is sufficiently unmistakable to indicate dependence of both the *Beowulf* and the sagas upon the same or similar Scandinavian sources.

The material, then, from which the story and setting of the *Beowulf* were fashioned was in its origin Continental. Of this alien and pagan material the Old English poet has shaped a poem courtly in mood, suggestive of epic tradition, and Christian in spirit. It is a mark of the poet's skill that the elements derived from these various and varied sources, from chronicle and legend, from folk-tale and lay, have been deftly integrated, and fused into a new unity.[3]

---

3. 'The whole must have succeeded admirably in creating in the minds of the poet's contemporaries the illusion of surveying a past, pagan but noble and fraught with a deep significance—a past that itself had depth and reached backward into a dark antiquity of sorrow. This impression of depth is an effect and a justification of the use of episodes and allusions to old tales, mostly darker, more pagan, and desperate than the foreground.' J.R.R.Tolkien, 'Beowulf: the monsters and the critics.' *Proceedings of the British Academy,* XXII, 1936, pp.270-71.

THE MANUSCRIPT

This 'book of the adventures of Beowulf' is contained in a manuscript volume now lodged in the British Museum, and known as *Cotton Vitellius, A. XV*. A combination of two once-separate codices, the manuscript contains nine Old English texts, four in the first codex, five in the second. The *Beowulf* (folios 129ª–198ᵇ) belongs to the second codex, in which it is preceded by three prose texts, and followed by the *Judith*. It represents the work of two scribes of the tenth century who were copying from an older manuscript, the first scribe writing out lines 1–1939; the second, the remainder of the poem. The text is not written as verse, but, as was then customary, in prose form; punctuation is sparse and uncertain; and there is no uniformity in the marking of long vowels. One gathers that the scribes were unlearned copyists, apparently not always understanding what they copied.

The *Beowulf* manuscript found its way, in the early seventeenth century, into the library of Sir Robert Cotton. The first recorded mention of the poem was made by Wanley in his famous *Catalogue* in 1705, but the terms he used were such as to suggest that he had not read the poem, for his Latin note misrepresents it as a tale of 'the wars which Beowulf, a certain Dane, sprung from the royal stock of the Scyldings, waged against chieftains of Sweden.'

From 1712 to 1730 the Cotton library was lodged in Essex House in the Strand. The purchase of Ashburnham House, Westminster, by the Government in 1730 provided a new housing for the books and manuscripts of the famous collection. It was here that a disastrous fire broke out in 1731 which consumed almost all the printed books, and destroyed or injured about 200 of 958 manuscripts. Unfortunately the

Beowulf manuscript was among those injured. Its edges, scorched by the fire, were rendered brittle and subject to progressive deterioration.

It is a matter of good fortune that in 1787 Thorkelin, a Danish scholar, made a transcript of the text of the *Beowulf*, and later in the year had a second transcript made for him. Upon these transcripts he based the first printed edition of the *Beowulf* in 1815. Subsequent collation by Thorpe and Kemble of the text of this edition with the *Beowulf* manuscript showed that in the process of deterioration words and letters, visible when the Thorkelin transcripts were made, had become illegible or had disappeared. Ultimately steps were taken to preserve the manuscript from further disintegration, each leaf being separately inlaid, and the whole rebound. In 1882, under the auspices of the Early English Text Society, an autotype edition of the manuscript was published, with a text by Zupitza based on the manuscript and on Thorkelin's transcripts.

THE NARRATIVE

The narrative element in the *Beowulf* consists of two stories, of separate origin, and unified only in the sense that Beowulf is the hero of both. Of these tales, the first represents an adventure of his youth in combat with two monsters; the second, his victorious but fatal battle in old age against a dragon. A long and prosperous reign over the Geats intervenes between the two exploits. The first episode involves the first 2199 lines of the *Beowulf*; the second, the remainder of the 3182 lines of the poem.

The story begins in the land of the Danes in the glorious reign of King Hrothgar. The power and splendor of his rule were symbolized in the great hall which he built and named

Heorot. The poet's statement that the light of this hall 'shone over many lands' may be taken as an index of the range and strength of Hrothgar's influence beyond his borders.

But time brought change. A horror came upon the land and the hall was haunted and ravaged by two monsters, male and female, of human shape but superhuman size, and of beastlike ferocity. The night raids upon Heorot by Grendel, the male, gradually diminished the number of Hrothgar's warriors and made the hall, as it towered up in the darkness, silent and deserted, a place of dread. For twelve years a superstitious terror lay like a shadow upon the land.

News of the calamity that afflicted the Danes spread far and wide, reaching at last the land of the Geats in southern Sweden, where it came to the ears of Beowulf. Against the advice of his uncle, Hygelac, the young adventurer, eager for fame, set sail for Denmark with a small band of followers to pit his courage and strength against the monsters, in the service of a friendly king.

The voyage of Beowulf to Denmark, the landing on foreign soil, the coast-guard's challenge, and the march inland to Heorot[4] are developed in swift-moving scenes, rich in color and in realistic detail. Gratefully welcomed by Hrothgar with royal entertainment in the hall, Beowulf and his band were entrusted with the task of freeing Heorot from the scourge of Grendel. There was one jarring note in the joyous ceremonial Unferth, a Danish courtier, jealous and proud, alluded to a swimming match between Beowulf and Breca, in which, he claimed, Breca had proved himself the better man. From this he prophesied an evil fate for Beowulf

4. The site of Heorot is somewhat generally identified by scholars with the modern village of Leire, standing about three miles from the coast on the island of Seeland. Cf. Chambers, *Beowulf, An Introduction*, pp.16-20.

if he dared to undertake encounter with Grendel. The reply of Beowulf and the realistic clash of personalities underlying the scene make this episode an outstanding passage of heightened dramatic tone.

At nightfall Beowulf and his men took over the hall, sleeping with their weapons at hand. They had not long to wait. Out of the mist and darkness Grendel burst in upon them, his eyes gleaming with a 'baleful light most like to flame.' Swiftly seizing one of the band, he tore him limb from limb, gulping down the flesh in huge morsels, 'even to the feet and hands.' Beowulf, who had made a vow that he would fight Grendel without weapon, closed with the monster in a grappling struggle that wrecked the ale-benches and shattered the woodwork of the hall. By virtue of his strength, he was able to inflict upon Grendel a fatal wound, wrenching his huge arm and claw out of the shoulder socket. With 'bloody tracks' the monster fled to the evil pool in the fen where he had his refuge, and, plunging in, sank to the depths. And there, says the poem, 'hell received him.'

With the coming of dawn Hrothgar and the Danes gathered at the hall, rejoicing as they viewed the huge claw of Grendel, and tracing the tracks that marked his flight to the fen. As they returned from the mere to Heorot with horses proudly prancing, a minstrel extemporized a song in praise of Beowulf's heroic deed, and chanted the lay of Sigemund's victory over a dragon. The hall was decked and a great feast prepared at which Hrothgar honored Beowulf and his men with many gifts, while the minstrel sang the lay of the fight at Finnsburg.

But the coming of night brought proof that the scourge had not been ended, nor the terror laid. The female monster, avenging the death of Grendel, raided the hall. In her

swift onset she slew Æschere, comrade and trusted coun-
sellor of Hrothgar, and bore off his body to the fen. The
Danes were heartsick with despair at this swift reprisal. But
Beowulf prepared again for battle, pledging Hrothgar that
he would avenge the death of Æschere. 'Better for man to
avenge a friend than much to mourn.'

The story of Beowulf's underwater fight against the troll-
wife in a huge cave at the bottom of the pool is marked by
a change in narrative mood. The poem in this section seems
to reveal intrusion, or survival, of fabulous elements in a
scene that in the narrative of the *Grettissaga* developed ele-
ments of realism. It is possible, of course, that the poet did
not fully understand his material, or interpreted as su-
pernatural, elements which the corresponding scene in the
Grettissaga makes natural and realistic. Whatever the expla-
nation, the reader will note in the descriptive passages of this
second episode an evident stress upon miracle and wonder.

The Danes and Geats together made their way to the mere.
The pool was in a dismal covert of trees that overhung gray
rock, and blood-stained water beneath. On the banks and in
the watery depths were snakelike monsters and strange sea-
drakes. And here the grief of the Danes was made bitter by
the sight of Æschere's severed head lying upon the brink.

Wearing helmet and byrny and bearing his sword, Beo-
wulf plunged into the pool. It was the space of a day before
he reached bottom. As he swam down, the water-monsters
beset him sorely with their menacing tusks. But fighting
them off he found himself at last in a great hall free of water,
and lighted with a glow as of firelight. Here he fought with
the savage water-hag. In his attack on her his sword failed
him, 'would not bite,' and he was forced to stake all on his
unaided strength. The troll-wife in a swift rush overthrew

him and, kneeling upon him, drew out her dagger. At this moment of impending defeat and death it was by divine aid that Beowulf regained his feet and seized an ancient sword from among the war-gear lying in the cave. Though the blade was heavy beyond the strength of other men, he struck with fury and slew the hag.

> The stout blade stabbed through her fated flesh;
> She sank in death; the sword was bloody.

The Danes, who held watch at the edge of the mere, seeing the waters suddenly stained with blood, believed that Beowulf had been killed, and despondently made their way back to the hall. The loyal Geats waited on. At last came Beowulf swimming up from the depths, bearing the ghastly head of Grendel and the ornamented hilt of the great sword whose blade had melted in the hag's venomous blood. Joyfully his followers gathered around him and accompanied him to Heorot. Four of them carried Grendel's head on a pike-staff, bearing it across the floor in the midst of the feasting, 'a terrible sight for lord and for lady.'

This final purging of the evil that had rested on Heorot Hrothgar celebrated by an elaborate feast with ceremonial speech and rich giving of gifts. Wealhtheow and the youthful Freawaru, wife and daughter of the king, graced the banquet with their presence. When the night shadows deepened and the feasting came to an end, the weary Beowulf was guided by a hall-thane to a place appointed, and there, with the great hall towering above him, his sleep was deep.

When the voice of the black-coated raven hailed the sunrise, and the time had come for Beowulf's return to his own country, Hrothgar bestowed upon him twelve gifts, and bade him a sad farewell.

> The peerless leader, the Scylding lord,
> Kissed the good thane and clasped to his bosom,
> While tears welled fast from the old man's eyes.
> Both chances he weighed in his wise, old heart,
> But greatly doubted if ever again
> They should meet in council, or drinking of mead.

The description of the return voyage to southern Sweden has elements of sea-realism which make the passage an appropriate parallel to the account of the earlier voyage to Denmark. Welcomed and feasted by Hygelac, Beowulf recounted his adventures among the Danes, and shared with King Hygelac and his queen, Hygd, the gifts which Hrothgar had given him. Hygelac in turn bestowed upon the hero an ancestral sword inherited from Hrethel, and honored Beowulf with a stately hall and seven thousand hides of land. So ends the first section of the narrative.

Between the slaying of the monsters and the killing of the dragon, many years intervened; more than fifty, if we take literally the poet's statement that Beowulf ruled for fifty winters.[5] In all probability, as used in this passage and a second time later in the poem,[6] the word 'fifty' is to be interpreted as a round number merely implying a long reign. No account is given, at this point in the text, of the circumstances of Beowulf's reign, aside from the general statement that he ruled well. The years are spanned and the dragon motif is introduced in a swift passage of twelve lines.

It is the nature of dragons, so the poet tells us, to hunt out buried treasure and guard the heathen gold. The dragon in *Beowulf* conforms to this tradition, having come upon a bur-

5. ll.2208-9.
6. l.2733.

ial treasure over which he brooded for three hundred years. Only when the hoard was plundered, and a precious cup carried off by the thief, was the wrath of the dragon roused and the destructiveness of his fury unloosed upon the land.

The account of the plundering of the hoard is not completely clear, since the text at this point is quite corrupt and requires extensive reconstruction.[7] One gathers that an outcast and fugitive, perhaps guilty of a crime and fleeing from punishment, in his flight blundered into the burial barrow, in which the dragon guarded his treasure. There from the hoarded riches he stole a cup which he carried back to his lord, perhaps as the price of forgiveness. Roused by the plundering of his barrow, the dragon began to ravage the land with flames and fury.

Beowulf prepared for battle against this menace to his people. Armed with his sword, Nægling, and an iron shield for defense against the fire of the monster, the king, with a small band, was guided by the thief to the dragon's earth-hall. Taking his stand near the stone entrance of the barrow and the hot stream that flowed from within, Beowulf shouted his challenge. The dragon, roused by the voice of man, came forth to the attack.

The struggle so begun is described in vigorous detail. The action divides into the three stages conventional in description of such a battle. Once more, as in his youthful adventure, the sword of Beowulf failed him; Nægling broke.

> It was not his lot that edges of iron
> Could help him in battle; his hand was too strong.

His shoulder-companions, who at the beginning had borne no part because Beowulf had wished to undertake the battle

7. ll.2221-31.

alone, in the hour of their lord's need turned and fled to the forest to save their lives. Only the youthful Wiglaf, son of Weohstan of the Wægmundings, remained to fight under the shield of his lord. In his third rush the dragon fastened his fangs in Beowulf's throat, dealing a deadly wound. Wiglaf repaid with a stout sword thrust; and Beowulf, with ebbing strength, drew his dagger and cut the worm in twain.

But the king had received his death-wound, and the end was near. To Wiglaf he gave his armor and rings, and wished him well in terms which seem to imply his succession to rule over the Geats:

> Heed well the needs, the wants of my people;
> My hour is come, and my end is near . . .
> You are the last of the Wægmunding line.
> All my kinsmen, earls in their glory,
> Fate has sent to their final doom;
> And I must follow.

It was a lonely death. Beowulf had no son to whom he could leave the succession, and only the lad, Wiglaf, was with him when death came. Somewhere in the background hovered the cowards who had deserted their king in his hour of need. It was Wiglaf who pronounced the curse upon the outcasts for their black disloyalty. It was Wiglaf who sat at the last alone with his fallen leader in the silence of the deathwatch, the living beside the dead.

A messenger proclaimed the news of Beowulf's fall, mingling the sad tidings with dark forebodings of war and disaster, now that the tribe had lost their king. The body of the dead dragon was tumbled over the cliff into the sea. In accordance with Beowulf's dying wish, a funeral pyre was built upon the headland, and a barrow constructed, destined

to be known by sailors from distant lands as Beowulf's Bar-
row. In it the dragon's treasure was once more buried, under
the earth of the headland, 'where it still remains as useless to
men as it was of yore.' On the brow of the cliff the greatest
of funeral fires was kindled, and the body of Beowulf burned.
Round the pyre rode his warriors mourning their fallen lord,
chanting their dirges, and proclaiming his virtue and fame.
A sense of Fate broods over these final scenes. A great and
noble king has fallen. The future looms dark and insecure.

SCANDINAVIAN AND ICELANDIC ANALOGUES

The supernatural forms of Grendel and Grendel's dam
are obviously derivative from folk-tale, though the *Beowulf*
poet in an early passage has blurred this lineage by tracing
their descent from the monstrous offspring of Cain. Grendel
is unusual among folk-tale monsters in bearing a name, and
the name itself furnishes a hint as to his primitive derivation.
The word Grendel, as Lawrence points out, can be associated
with the Old English *grund*, i.e. ground, bottom, or watery
depths, and it is significant that it is in just such depths that
we find the lurking-place of Grendel and his mother. Eng-
lish place-names preserve records of localities known as *gren-
dles mere* (the grendel's pool), *grindles bec* (the grendel's
brook), and *gryndeles sylle* (the grendel's swamp).[8] In these
place-names the word *grendel* seems to be used as a generic
term for a 'grendel,' or water-monster, and it is probable
that the water-demons of the *Beowulf* have original deriva-
tion from the waterfall trolls of Scandinavian myth.

More directly, however, the male and female monsters of
our poem, and the narrative of Beowulf's victories over
them, are traceable to well-defined and recurring patterns in

8. W.W.Lawrence, *Beowulf and Epic Tradition*, p.163.

a familiar type of European folk-tale. Frederick Panzer in 1910 published the results of a careful study of over two hundred folk-tales which have elements of resemblance to the Grendel story.[9] These tales, with all their variations of outline, have enough in common, in structure and detail, to indicate general conformance to a recurring type, which has come to be known as the tale of 'The Bear's Son.' The name is suggested by the bearlike attributes of the hero, who in some versions of the tale is actually the son, or the fosterling, of a bear. Vestigial traces of this element are to be noted in the *Beowulf* in the superhuman strength of the hero, and the bearlike wrestling of his fight with Grendel, and later with Dæghrefn, the slayer of Hygelac.

From the varying versions of the tale of 'The Bear's Son,' something like a central frame, or outline, can be reconstructed. An aged king builds a hall or house which is nightly haunted by a demon. The elder sons of the king are unable to overcome the invader, but the youngest son, formerly held in little esteem, wrestles with the monster and wounds him. The flight of the demon is marked by a trail of blood. An episode follows in which the hero fights in an underground lair of monsters, often against a male and a female. His victory over them, sometimes by use of a magic sword, frees captive maidens who return to the upper world. But the hero is abandoned by faithless companions, and must single-handed invent means of escape from the monster's home. The tale often ends with the punishment of the traitors and the marriage of the hero with one of the rescued maidens.

Similarities in this outline to the Grendel episodes of the *Beowulf* are, of course, general rather than precise. But it

9. F.Panzer, *Studien zur germanischen Sagengeschichte*, München, 1910.

seems clear that Panzer is correct in suggesting that a relationship exists, and that the *Beowulf* narrative in this respect had its earliest origin in the crude substance of folk-tale. The details of similarity suggest themselves at once: the building of the hall, the nightly invasion of the monster, the fact that the hero was little esteemed in youth,[10] the nature of the fight and the monster's wound, the trail of blood, the female monster, the fight in the cave under water, the magic sword, the desertion of the hero by comrades.[11]

Even more specific resemblance, however, exists between the *Beowulf* and certain Scandinavian sagas. The Icelandic saga of Grettir the Strong, dating from the end of the thirteenth century, has elements which resemble the *Beowulf* material and, in the account of the fight under water, throw a revealing light on uncertainties of description in the *Beowulf* account. It is not probable that the Sandhills episode in the *Grettissaga* was based upon the *Beowulf*, but rather that both stories were independently developed from more primitive Scandinavian origins.

According to the *Grettissaga* a hall at a place called Sandhills had for some time been ravaged by the nightly raids of a monster. The master of the house and subsequently a housecarle had disappeared. Hearing of these depredations, on Yule-eve Grettir the Strong undertook a watch in the hall. Toward midnight a huge troll-wife burst in and Grettir struggled with her in a furious wrestling match which wrecked everything in the hall even to the cross-paneling. The troll-wife dragged him out of the hall and down to the river bank where Grettir succeeded in freeing his right hand, and with his short sword smote off the monster's arm at the

---

10. For traces of this motif in *Beowulf*, see ll.2183-8.
11. In *Beowulf*, by the Danes, ll.1600-02.

shoulder. Thereupon she fell into the river and was washed down the force.

In the second episode Grettir led the local priest, who doubted the tale, to the scene of his victory over the hag. From the river brink they beheld a cave deep under the cliff, and the water flowing over it. Leaving the priest guarding a rope fastened to a peg, Grettir dived down under the falling torrent, and came up in a great cave in which a fire was burning. Here he fought with a giant and smote out his entrails so that the stream was colored by his blood. When the priest beheld the bloodstained water, he judged that Grettir had been killed and, leaving the rope fastened to its peg, returned home. Grettir found in the cave the bones of the two men who had disappeared. Carrying the bones in a bag, and a carved rune-staff, he made his way to the rope. Shaking it and finding the priest gone, he drew himself up through the force by main strength, and returned with the bones and the rune-staff to the church porch.

One need not elaborate in this account the many details of resemblance to the *Beowulf* material. Except for the fact that the *Grettissaga* reverses the order of conflict, the first struggle being with the female, the similarity of the two accounts in important detail is close, and clearly indicates a genetic relation between the two narratives. In one respect there is inconsistence, and this variance is itself suggestive. Grettir's entrance into the cave behind the waterfall by diving through the force and his return by pulling himself up through the water by a rope suggest for the second episode of the Sandhills story a landscape-setting intelligible and realistic. It is probable that in this respect the Icelandic narrative, in spite of its later date, has more faithfully preserved primitive realism. The recourse to the supernatural in the corresponding scene of the *Beowulf* would seem to represent either inability of the Old English poet to visualize realistically the landscape which served as setting for the battle, or a transformation and blurring of primitive conceptions by literary influence and epic convention.

Lawrence has pointed out another interesting analogue to the underwater fight in the *Beowulf*.[12] This parallel is found in an episode in the saga of Samson the Fair. In the account there given of a fight between Samson and a female troll who dwelt behind a waterfall, there are resemblances to details in the *Grettissaga* episode, and in the blurred descriptions of the corresponding scene in the *Beowulf*. The fight takes place in a cave behind a waterfall; the hero dives through the force to reach the cave; the water of the stream is stained with the she-troll's blood; and the waiting Gallyn decides that the hero has been killed.

Other episodes may be cited, from Scandinavian saga, which seem to suggest general resemblance to the *Beowulf*, as in the Glamr episode of the *Grettissaga*, and Orm's victories over a female demon in cat form, and a giant called Brusi, in the tale of Orm Storolfsson. But the resemblances are certainly less sharp and conclusive than are those in the Sandhills episode of the *Grettissaga*.

In various versions of this folk-tale material we catch hints of slow processes of reworking and reshaping which help to explain certain forms the material has assumed in the *Beowulf*. The fact that Beowulf, after his victory over Grendel's dam, cuts off the head of the dead Grendel[13] would seem to be a

---

12. 'Beowulf and the Saga of Samson the Fair,' *Studies in English Philology, A Miscellany in honor of Frederick Klaeber*, 172–81; also, *Beowulf and Epic Tradition*, 188–91.

13. ll. 1588–90.

surviving trace from those stories in which the male mon-
ster is actually slain in the underwater struggle. The state-
ment of the poem that Beowulf in youth was little esteemed[14]
may well reflect the primitive tradition which made the hero
of these battles against monsters a younger son, considered
unworthy, who succeeded after his elder brothers had failed.
The scene in the *Beowulf* in which the Danes, beholding the
bloodstained water, leave the margin of the pool and return
home, though Beowulf's own men remain,[15] may have taken
its form from vague reminiscence of versions of the tale in
which the hero is deserted by his comrades.

In one respect, the most noteworthy of Scandinavian ana-
logues is the saga of Hrolf Kraki. In many ways this rather
clumsily told tale of the fourteenth century is not as close
to the *Beowulf* as is the *Grettissaga* or even, in certain respects,
the *Samsonssaga*. But it is significant and important that in
the tale of Hrolf Kraki, as in the *Beowulf*, the theme of a
land delivered by a foreign hero from the ravages of a mon-
ster is inserted into a historical pattern. In both the *Hrolfssaga*
and the *Beowulf* the crude substance of folk-tale has been
elevated in dignity and set in a frame of chronicle. The Hrol
of the saga is identical with the Hrothulf of the *Beowulf*. In-
deed, in Scandinavian chronicle it was the reign of Hrolf
(Hrothulf) rather than that of Hroar (Hrothgar) which stood
out as an era of glory and splendor. The popular legend was
the legend of the heroic greatness of Hrolf. It is, therefore,
not altogether surprising to find the tale of the slaying of the
monster by Bothvarr Bjarki attached to the saga of Hrolf
Kraki.

If the *Hrolfssaga* is set over against the *Beowulf* a corre-

14. ll.2183-8.
15. ll.1600-05.

spondence is clear. The heroic service which Bothvarr Bjarki
performs for Hrolf is similar to the heroic service which
Beowulf performs for Hrothgar. And attending this chief
correspondence there are, as Klaeber points out,[16] additional
similarities of detail. The name Bjarki, like the name Beo-
wulf, suggests the bear attributes of the hero of the folk-tale.
Bothvarr comes to Denmark from Gautland where his
brother is ruler; Beowulf from Geatland where his uncle is
king. Bothvarr's quarrel with the king's warriors when he
first comes to court suggests the Unferth episode in *Beowulf*.
There are, however, discrepancies. In the *Hrolfssaga* there is
one monster, not two, and that monster a winged creature,
apparently of the dragon type, and in no way suggestive of
Grendel, or Grendel's dam, of the *Beowulf*. Nevertheless, the
resemblances between the *Hrolfssaga* and the *Beowulf*, in gen-
eral pattern and structure, cannot be disregarded, and it seems
probable that the *Hrolfssaga* represents, in later and gro-
tesquely transformed tradition, the same fusion of folk-tale
and chronicle that underlay the Old English epic. That there
is a fundamental identity of Beowulf and Bothvarr Bjarki is
unmistakably suggested by the Icelandic ballads in which
Bothvarr aids Athils in battle against Ali, as Beowulf aids
Eadgils against Onela.[17]

It is not possible to trace the dragon fight of the *Beowulf*
to specific sources or analogues. There are certain details in
Saxo's account of Frotho's battle with a dragon[18] which
somewhat resemble details in the Old English poem, and
those who find these resemblances convincing explain the
puzzling use of *ealond* in the *Beowulf*[19] by its correspondence

16. *Beowulf*, Introduction, p.xix.
17. ll.2391–6
18. *Gesta Danorum*, ii,38.
19. l.2334.

to the *island* of Saxo's narrative. But, many dragons have wound their way through the pages of medieval legend, and for much of the incidental detail relating to Beowulf's dragon broad and general correspondences are to be found in various versions of the dragon myth.

It is, however, significant that the assignment of the *Beowulf* dragon to the guarding of burial treasure is in accord with ideas of the nature and attributes of dragons as set forth in the Old English *Gnomic Verses*: 'The dragon lieth on the grave-mound, old, exultant in treasure.' It is a grave-mound and a burial treasure that have become the concern of the *Beowulf* dragon. The description of the dragon's barrow suggests somewhat precisely a type of ancient European burial mound. These mounds, constructed of earth, completely covered an inner burial chamber and entrance passage, which were built of huge slabs of stone. The opening into the passage could be closed with stone slabs, blocking entrance into the mound. In the *Beowulf* the dragon had found the mound 'standing open.' The various references in the poem to the dragon's earth-hall, or barrow,[20] are sufficiently detailed to indicate beyond doubt that it was such a burial mound the poet had in mind, and even to warrant conjecture that the description may have been based on actual observation.

Two widely differing accounts of the origin of the buried treasure are set forth in the poem: the first, in an extended elegiac passage;[21] the second, in a briefer statement near the end of the poem.[22] According to the first account, a whole race of men had perished, dwindling until one solitary survivor held the accumulated wealth of the clan. Lonely of

20. ll.2212-3, 2232, 2271, 2410, 2515, 2718ff.
21. ll.2231-70.
22. ll.3051-75.

heart and grieving for the dead past, he buried the treasure in a newly built barrow, recommitting the gold to the ground with an invocation of Earth itself:

> Keep thou, O Earth, what men could not keep—
> This costly treasure—it came from thee!

The lines of which these are the prelude include some of the finest elegiac verse in Old English poetry, and employ skillfully themes and imagery characteristic of such Northumbrian elegies as the *Wanderer* and the *Ruin*.[23]

The origin of the buried treasure, as set forth in the second passage, is quite different. In this instance, the treasure had been buried in the earth by illustrious princes of old, with magic spells and a curse to protect it from invasion. As the implications of the passage are reconstructed by Lawrence, 'illustrious chieftains buried the gold, with spells to protect it, pronouncing a curse upon those who should disturb it. When the hoard was plundered, the curse operated immediately; the dragon began his fearful ravages.'[24] Of these two accounts, so apparently in conflict, it seems probable that the second is the older. In such instances of variance we catch glimpses of the processes of growth and transformation by which the material of our poem has been shaped: slow accumulation of legend, tradition upon tradition; incomplete fusion of material stratified as to age and source.

One of the most dramatic elements in the description of Beowulf's struggle with the dragon is the noteworthy depiction of *comitatus* spirit memorably personalized in the figure of Wiglaf. The youth of the lad, his heroic courage, his contempt for the cowards who have deserted their lord,

---

23. See Kennedy, *Old English Elegies*, Introduction.
24. *Beowulf and Epic Tradition*, p.215.

and his hero-worshipping devotion to Beowulf combine to suggest in striking manner the Germanic imperative of unconditional loyalty to overlord and king. It has been frequently noted that there are similarities between the Wiglaf scenes in the *Beowulf* and the Byrhtnoth episode in the *Battle of Maldon*, similarities which extend to detail and, in one instance, to almost identical phrasing of the 'boast-words' of Beowulf and Leofsunu. Such parallelism can hardly be accidental. Carleton Brown, in a recent study of the relation of the *Beowulf* to the seventeenth *Blickling Homily*, inclines to the view that, in the late tenth century, in the *Maldon* as in the *Blickling Homily*, we have to do with passages modified and shaped by reminiscence of the *Beowulf*.[25]

The joining of the dragon fight to the Grendel material furnishes illustration of the poetic shaping that has transformed the primitive materials of folk-tale and chronicle into completed epic narrative. The story of the heroic Beowulf must be rounded out to his death. And the death must be worthy, a death in battle, but in noble battle. The material of the dragon myth lay ready at hand. Elements of the supernatural in the myth made battle with the dragon heroic, and death glorious. More important, the death of Beowulf is set forth as the death not of a great king only, but of a good king. The idealism of youthful adventure had matured into the sober virtues of a ruler whose life expressed the best of his age: concern for his people, regard for his word, the preference of peace over war, the desire for fame.

The artistry of a tale can be judged by its ending. The narrative of the *Beowulf* has worthy conclusion in its final scene, a 'set-piece' of outstanding excellence. The funeral of Beowulf has elements that suggest comparison with similar

25. *PMLA*, LIII, 905-16.

burial scenes of classical epic.[26] The burning of the body, the building of the barrcw, the formal devotion of armor and trophies, the dirges and elegiac laments are familiar detail of burial ceremonial reflecting the customs of the Heroic Age. It is possible that the descriptions in the *Beowulf* may reflect Gothic custom as reported by Jordanes in his account of the funeral of Attila.[27] The warriors of Beowulf, who rode about his barrow chanting his virtues and mourning his death, suggest the horsemen of Attila who rode 'in a circle' round his body with 'a lay of lamentation.' But it is to be noted that very much the same custom seems to be indicated in the description of the burning of the dead in the Eleventh Book of the *Aeneid*:[28] 'Thrice, girt in glittering arms, they have marched about the blazing piles, thrice compassed on horseback the sad fire of death and uttered their wail.'

HISTORICAL BACKGROUNDS

The narrative of the youthful heroism and the last battle and death of Beowulf, rooted, as we have seen, in the primitive material of folk-tale, is skillfully projected against a background of history and chronicle. The historical material in the poem is not set forth in connected sequence, but is present in passages of allusion, reminiscent or foreshadowing. Though the course of historic incident, if reconstructed from the *Beowulf* alone, is not always clear or complete, comparison with analogous material in Scandinavian and Icelandic saga and chronicle will often supplement and clarify the historical elements of the Old English epic. In general the allu-

---

26. *Aeneid*, VI, 179-235; XI, 182-212. See also *Iliad* XXIII, 138ff.; XXIV, 785ff.; *Odyssey*, XXIV, 43ff.

27. *De Origine Actibusque Getarum*, XLIX, 12.

28. *Aeneid*, XI, 182-212.

sions in the *Beowulf* have to do with the civil dissensions, the tragic and bitter feuds, which characterize the chronicles of the Geats and the Danes. The use of this material has, of course, essential appropriateness in an epic narrative in which the two principal figures, Beowulf and Hrothgar, were respectively of Geatish and Danish blood.

The *Beowulf*, then, suggests, in somewhat shadowy outline, the fateful history of two dynasties, the glories of great kings, and their tragedies of violence and blood. The opening verses of the poem stress the splendor of the Danish line. As the story begins, Hrothgar, son of Healfdene, and fourth in the line of Scylding succession, held the throne. The fame of his rule was widespread, and the light of Heorot, his great council hall, 'shone over many lands.' His queen, Wealhtheow, lady of the Helmings, holds no minor position in the poem, but plays her part with dignity and grace in the established ceremonial of the court.

But seeds of dissension had been sown, and foreshadowing of tragic event now and again darkens the lines of the poem. The succession from Healfdene should have descended through Heorogar, the eldest son, to Heorogar's son, Heoroweard. But Heoroweard had been passed over, and Hrothgar, his uncle, had succeeded to power. The reasons that had led to this apparent usurpation are not made clear. Some dim light, perhaps, is thrown upon the matter by Hrothgar's gift to Beowulf of Heorogar's armor.[29] Such alienation of his father's war-gear should normally have been considered a disgrace to Heoroweard. But Hrothgar intimates that it had been Heorogar's own wish that his armor should not descend to his son. Whatever of justice, or injustice, may lie hidden behind this extraordinary incident, the slighted and

29. ll.2155–62.

neglected Heoroweard is a figure of the tragic background, biding his time, and in the end winning a short-lived revenge.

It is Heoroweard's cousin, Hrothulf, son of Halga, who throughout the poem holds a place of honor at court, living on apparently friendly terms with Hrothgar and the king's sons, Hrethric and Hrothmund. But there are passages in the poem which seem to imply uneasiness on the part of the king and queen as to the fate which might befall their sons when Hrothgar's death should leave them vulnerable. Wealhtheow, it is true, expresses her confidence that Hrothulf will favor and protect Hrethric and Hrothmund

> if he bears in mind
> The many honors and marks of love
> We bestowed upon him when he still was a boy.[30]

But the very qualification of the remark seems to intimate suspicion and fear, and this may explain the earnestness of Wealhtheow's request that Beowulf befriend her sons with counsel and help. It may have been a similar uneasiness in Hrothgar's mind that led to his adoption of Beowulf as foster son,[31] and to Beowulf's assurance that, should Hrethric ever have reason to come to the Geatish court, he would find there a multitude of friends.[32]

Whatever the degree of foreshadowing in such passages, the Scandinavian analogues make it clear that after Hrothgar's death Hrothulf took arms against Hrethric, slew him, and seized the throne.[33] But his treachery was not to go un-

---

30. ll.1185-7.   31. ll.946-50.   32. ll.1836-9.

33. Kemp Malone ('Hrethric,' *PMLA*, xlii, 268-313) suggests an ingenious outline of Hrothulf-Hrethric relations. Malone brings evidence from Scandinavian sources into relation with the *Beowulf* to indicate that Hrethric for a time actually held the Danish throne, having driven Hrothulf out of power, only in turn to be overthrown again by Hrothulf.

avenged. The long-brooding, slighted Heoroweard struck at last. With a small following of Danes augmented by a Swedish force, he attacked and killed Hrothulf and set fire to the hall. But in the very moment of triumph, and in the act of receiving the oath of homage, Heoroweard was stabbed to death by a surviving follower of Hrothulf, and amid the smoke of the burning hall the Scylding dynasty came to its end.

Side by side with the allusions in the *Beowulf* to this chain of dissension and treachery, there is more extended reference to the bitter and bloody feud which the Danes waged with their neighbors, the Heathobards. The origin of the feud apparently dated from the reign of Healfdene, who was slain by Froda, king of the Heathobards. The Danes in turn avenged Healfdene's fall, killing Froda and burning his hall. It was at this stage that Hrothgar proposed to compose the feud by the betrothal of his daughter, Freawaru, to Froda's son, Ingeld.

The betrothal of Freawaru permits the poet to develop one of the most dramatic themes inherent in this historical material. A passage in Beowulf's narrative of his Danish adventures[34] expresses his foreboding that, in spite of Hrothgar's diplomacy, the feud is certain to flare up with renewed bitterness. Beowulf foresees that when Ingeld shall lead his lady into hall she will be attended by a Dane wearing sword and armor which had been taken as spoil in battle with the Heathobards. The son of the slain and despoiled Heathobard, angered by this affront, is incited to revenge by an older warrior who uses the opportunity to awaken the ancient feud.

34. ll.2024-69.

Do you see, my lord, the sword of your father,
The blade he bore to the last of his fights,
The pride of his heart, as under his helmet
The Scyldings slew him, the savage Danes,
When Withergyld fell, and after the slaughter,
The fall of heroes, they held the field?
And now a son of those bloody butchers,
Proud in his trappings, tramps into hall
And boasts of the killing, clothed with the treasure
That is yours by your birthright to have and to hold?[35]

Heathobard resentment, thus fanned into flame, brought bitter renewal of the feud, and in the end Ingeld led an invading force which stormed Heorot and attacked Hrothgar. The Old English *Widsith*[36] gives a brief record of the defeat and slaughter of the Heathobards in this battle: 'For a long time,' we are told, 'Hrothwulf and Hrothgar, nephew and uncle, kept peace with one another after they had driven off the Viking race, crushing the attack of Ingeld and hacking down in Heorot the Heathobard host.' Ingeld apparently died in the battle, and of the youthful Freawaru, so woefully enmeshed in this web of tragic fate, we hear no more.[37]

There are few passages in the *Beowulf* which strike a more dramatic note than this story of the aged warrior whose repeated incitement inflames to vengeance the humiliated son, and pours out in renewed bloodshed all the rancors of the ancient feud. It is dramatic narrative done with relish and vigor, and may well have its kinship to those songs of Ingeld

35. ll.2047-56.
36. *Widsith*, 45-9.
37. For detailed discussion of the story of Ingeld see Kemp Malone, 'Swerting,' *The Germanic Review*, XIV, 1939, pp.235-57.

for love of which Alcuin once rebuked the Northumbrian monks.[38]

A somewhat detached figure, a certain King Heremod, whose position in the Danish line is by no means clear, is twice[39] prominently mentioned in the *Beowulf* in terms which indicate that legends of his life and rule afforded familiar material for poetic use. The *Anglo-Saxon Chronicle* lists Heremod as the father of Scyld, the founder of the Scylding line. In spite of this suggestion of myth, the story of Heremod has obvious elements of realism, and it is a matter of interest that his name has the H alliteration characteristic of the Scylding dynasty. Whatever his position in the line of succession, he seems to have been widely known for his deeds of violence, and for lack of that generosity which the *comitatus* ideal required of a noble lord and leader.

References in Saxo to the father of Scyld, there called Lotherus, seem to throw light upon the story of Heremod. It would appear that it was after an elder brother had proved incompetent that Heremod seized the throne and ruled the Danes. But his vices speedily disclosed themselves. He was guilty of slaying comrades in drunken rage, and of lack of generosity toward loyal followers. Driven from power in the end, he seems to have furnished a stock *exemplum* of unworthy rule, and Hrothgar's homiletic speech,[40] shortly before Beowulf's departure, urges him to avoid Heremod's vices, and to learn from Heremod's fate.

Those passages in the *Beowulf* which deal with the chroni-

38. 'Quid Hinieldus cum Christo? Angusta est domus; utrosque tenere non poterit.'

39. ll.901, 1709.

40. ll.1700–84.

cles of the Geats and their constant wars with the Swedes
are somewhat less clear than the poet's treatment of the
Scylding dynasty and, except for the fine passage on the
battle of Ravenswood[41] and the elegiac lines suggested by the
death of Herebeald,[42] less dramatic. Beowulf is portrayed, in
his later years, as king of the Geats; indeed, he is represented
in the poem as the great king of that dynasty. But it is nota-
ble that his name does not alliterate with H, as is character-
istic of the names of the kings who preceded him, Hrethel,
Hæthcyn, Hygelac, and Heardred. Evidently, as the mate-
rial of the poem took shape, he was inserted into the Geat
succession and, in this respect, has been drafted from folk-
tale into chronicle. Lawrence finds him less convincing as a
figure of chronicle than as a hero of folk-tale. 'Beowulf con-
stantly betrays his origin as a folk-tale hero. A certain un-
reality surrounds him as king; he is more at his ease as a
slayer of monsters.'[43]

Within the range of our poem, the royal line of the Geats
may be said to have begun with Hrethel. His reign was
darkened, and his old age embittered, by one of those trage-
dies which from time to time gave such dramatic pathos to
legends and chronicles of Germanic life. Hrethel had three
sons, Herebeald, Hæthcyn, and Hygelac. Herebeald died be-
fore his father, accidentally slain by an arrow from Hæth-
cyn's bow. Such a death created for Hrethel the most tragic
situation that could grow from the customs of the Germanic
feud, involving, as it did, an irreconcilable conflict of loyal-
ties. It was his duty to avenge Herebeald's death. But duty

41. ll.2922–99.
42. ll.2444–62.
43. *Beowulf and Epic Tradition*, p.87.

and loyalty alike withheld him from taking vengeance upon his own son.

A fine elegiac passage in the *Beowulf* springs directly from this incident. The poet, in his treatment of the theme, describes an aged father who, like Hrethel, mourned for a son killed under circumstances which precluded revenge:[44]

> In the house of his son he gazes in sorrow
> On wine-hall deserted and swept by the wind,
> Empty of joy. The horsemen and heroes
> Sleep in the grave. No sound of the harp,
> No welcoming revels as often of old!
> He goes to his bed with his burden of grief;
> To his spirit it seems that dwelling and land
> Are empty and lonely, lacking his son.[45]

It was in this mood that Hrethel mourned for Herebeald. His days and nights were shadowed by this tragic sorrow, and in the end he died of a broken heart.

The bitter wars between the Geats and the Swedes seem to have begun in the reign of Hæthcyn as a result of attacks on the Geats made by Onela and Ohthere, sons of Ongentheow, the Swedish king. In revenge Hæthcyn led an invading force against the Swedes, captured Ongentheow's queen, and fought a pitched battle with the Swedish force near the forest of Ravenswood. This battle is mentioned near the end of the *Beowulf* where the description has marked dramatic relevancy, occurring, as it does, in a speech which prophesies renewal of the Swedish feud as a result of Beowulf's death.

44. See '*Beowulf* 2444-2471,' D. Whitelock, *Medium Aevum*, VIII, No.3, 1939, pp.198-204.
45. ll.2455-62.

In the battle of Ravenswood, as described in the *Beowulf*,[46] Ongentheow slew Hæthcyn and rescued the Swedish queen. He drove the wearied forces of the Geats into the forest where he held them through the night hemmed in and helpless:

All the long hours of the night he thundered his threats
That some on the morrow he would slay with the edge of
   the sword,
And some should swing on the gallows as food for the fowls.

But hope returned with dawn when the hard-pressed Geats heard the horn of Hygelac, and the trumpets of the troops he brought to their aid. The stronghold to which Ongentheow withdrew was stormed and taken by the Geats, and in the struggle Ongentheow was killed by two brothers, Wulf and Eofor. Eofor's heroism was rewarded by marriage with the only daughter of Hygelac.[47]

During the lull in the Swedish wars which followed, Hygelac embarked upon the famous expedition against the Franks in which he lost his life. This raid, probably to be dated about 516, is described in Gregory's *Historia Francorum,* and in the *Liber Historiae Francorum,* and is repeatedly mentioned in the *Beowulf.*[48] Hygelac was successful in the initial attack, devastating the land, taking prisoners, and loading his ships with spoil. But before he could embark he was attacked by Theoderic's son, Theodebert, and killed. His

46. ll.2922-99

47. Girvan shows that the tradition of this marriage involves implications as to the ages of Hygelac and Hygd difficult to reconcile with details given, or implied, elsewhere in the poem. The statement as to the marriage, therefore, must be regarded with some suspicion. See R.Girvan, *Beowulf and the Seventh Century,* pp.71-3.

48. ll.1202-14; 2354-68; 2501-8; 2913-21.

fleet of ships was defeated in a naval battle, and the captured booty recovered by the Franks. Certain lines of the *Beowulf*[49] reflect, even in this material of chronicle, the fabulous nature of legends that clustered around Beowulf's name. After slaying Dæghrefn, who had killed his uncle, he made his way to the shore with thirty suits of armor on his back, and escaped by swimming the sea-stretches from Friesland to southern Sweden.

After Hygelac's death his queen, Hygd, offered the rule to Beowulf, having no hope, as we learn from the poem,[50] that her young son, Heardred, could defend the land against foreign foes. Beowulf refused the offer, but undertook to serve as protector until the youthful Heardred should come of age.[51]

During Heardred's reign, war with the Swedes once more broke out.[52] The cause of the renewal is not altogether clear. Apparently, in some manner, the nephews of the Swedish king Onela, his brother Ohthere's sons, Eanmund and Eadgils, had become involved in a conspiracy against Onela. The conspiracy had failed, and they had taken refuge among the Geats under the protection of Heardred. In revenge Onela attacked the Geats. Eanmund was slain, Eadgils fled, and Heardred lost his life in defending the exiled Swedish princes.

With Heardred's death the rule passed to Beowulf, and there seems to have been an interval of peace. But later, the

49. ll.2354-68.
50. ll.2369-72.
51. We can not be sure whether Hygd, 'daughter of Hæreth,' was a historical figure, though there are touches of realism in the poet's description of her. Her youth is stressed, and her fineness of nature. The poet takes opportunity to introduce, in contrast to Hygd, the figure of Thryth and the allusion to the tale of Offa, which is the one bit of Anglian tradition in *Beowulf*.
52. ll.2379-90.

poem tells us,[53] Eadgils made a second attempt on the Swedish throne in a war in which he had strong support from Beowulf, and in which he was successful. Thereafter, during Beowulf's long reign, there is no hint of further trouble between the Geats and the Swedes. But as the poem comes to its close, with Beowulf dead and his power ended, the minds of the Geats are filled with dark forebodings of a renewal of this ancient intertribal feud.

These then are the themes of tribal tradition, the tragic legends of violence and fate, borrowings from which are interwoven with transcript of folkway and epic invention to shape a frame for the fabulous tales of Beowulf's triumph over monster and dragon. The interweaving of these strains of chronicle, legend, and folk-tale must have been a process of gradual fusion through long years of tradition. But the poet's skill in control of this traditional material is displayed throughout the poem. The allusions are sufficiently central and sharp to suggest the historic background, and, where the nature of the material has invited more extended poetic development, the poem has been enriched by deft and artful use of these themes. The story of Ingeld, the lines on Heremod, the elegiac portrait of Hrethel mourning for his son, and the dramatic description of the fight at Ravenswood, all serve to provide background and perspective. The material of tribal history and tribal legend is employed to heighten action, and to adorn the telling of an epic tale.

THE SIGEMUND LAY

Rich in dramatic appeal, but uncertain and puzzling in many of its details, is the material of Germanic legend found in the songs of Hrothgar's minstrel. The morning after Beo-

53. ll.2391-6.

wulf's fight with Grendel, as Hrothgar and his retainers re-
turn from Grendel's mere, the minstrel celebrates Beowulf's
heroism, and weaves into his song the tale of Sigemund's
triumph over a dragon. Later, the hall is decorated and a
feast held, in the course of which the minstrel chants the lay
of Finn. In the Sigemund lay the actual words of the min-
strel's song are not given; the substance is set forth in sum-
mary or paraphrase. In the Finnsburg lay the method is more
doubtful, and it is possible that the poet is setting down the
lay as the minstrel is supposed to have sung it.

In both songs there is happy choice of material. The honor
implied by the linking of Beowulf with the heroic Sige-
mund of the Volsungs was gracious and felicitous praise. The
tale of the swift and terrible vengeance which the Danes
visited upon their foes at Finnsburg was a direct appeal to
tribal pride, furnishing fitting material for rehearsal at a
gathering of the clan.

The allusive nature of the references in the Sigemund lay
to the heroic exploits of Sigemund and Sinfjötli, and to
Sigemund's victory over a dragon, indicate that the poet
was able to assume acquaintance on the part of his readers
with the primitive material from which was shaped the
Volsungasaga, the dramatic northern legend to which the
Middle High German *Nibelungenlied* has relationship. The
Volsungasaga represents Sigemund as the eldest of ten sons
of Volsungr, king of the Huns. Sigemund's twin sister,
Signy, was the wife of King Siggeir of Gautland. On a visit
to Siggeir's court, Volsungr and his men were treacherously
set upon and slain, and his sons captured and killed, one by
one. Sigemund alone, by Signy's help, escaped and took up
his dwelling in the forest. Sigemund and Signy thereafter
devoted themselves to planning vengeance for the treacher-

ous wrong done their house. When Signy's two sons by Siggeir were old enough, they were sent to Sigemund that he might test their courage and try if they were worthy to aid him. Being found unworthy, both were killed.

In the end convinced that only one of pure Volsung strain could succeed in the heroic task, Signy, in the guise of a witch, visited Sigemund and received shelter for the night. In due time she bore Sigemund a son whom she named Sinfjötli. When he reached ten years, Signy sent him to join Sigemund, and from him receive training in courage and endurance. Sometimes as men, sometimes as werewolves, Sigemund and Sinfjötli roamed the forests together, comrades in many perilous exploits. After the boy came of age, the two comrades joined in an attack on the hall of Siggeir, and set fire to it in the night. Siggeir and his men perished, and with them Signy who, having obtained vengeance, refused to live. 'So much have I done to accomplish revenge that it is now in no wise possible for me to live; I will die gladly with Siggeir, the king, though I married him by compulsion.' So ran the tale of the Volsung revenge.

The use made in the *Beowulf* of this primitive material is brief and partial. The borrowing is most recognizable in the account there given of the heroic adventures of Sinfjötli and Sigemund. Sinfjötli appears in the poem as Fitela, and is referred to as the nephew of Sigemund. It may be that we have here a reflection of the tradition that until the events of the final catastrophe Sigemund remained ignorant that Sinfjötli was his own son. The achievement of Signy's revenge is not touched upon in the *Beowulf* save as the figure of Sinfjötli is symbolic of her purpose.[54]

54. In this connection it is interesting to note that an Old English strophic poem, once considered the *First Riddle*, was in 1902 interpreted by Schofield

The theme of Sigemund's fight with a dragon is found nowhere outside of the *Beowulf*. The great dragon fight of the *Volsungasaga* is fought, not by Sigemund, but by Sigurd, the posthumous son of Sigemund. There is, moreover, no very close correspondence between the details of Sigurd's battle with Fafnir, and the description in the *Beowulf* of Sigemund's exploit. Sigemund's victory is set forth as one in a series of heroic exploits in which, in all instances but this, Sigemund and Sinfjötli had engaged together. 'Very many of the race of giants they had slain with the sword.' There follows immediately the account of Sigemund and the dragon, and the statement that in this battle Sigemund was fighting alone. 'Fitela was not with him.'

The *Beowulf* passage includes a reference to the dragon's hoard.[55] The dragon is called *hordes hyrde,* the 'guardian of the hoard,' and Sigemund, after his victory, loads a sea-boat with jewels and treasure. But no reference is made to the origin or past history of the hoard, nor is anything said of the curse that, in the *Volsungasaga,* the dwarf, Andvari, lays upon it. On the whole, Sigemund's dragon fight, as set forth in the *Beowulf,* is too summarized and allusive to suggest to a modern reader the background of legend which the poet had in mind. The more sophisticated elements of the later *Volsungasaga* episode are quite lacking, and the narrative as we have it suggests a simpler and more heroic motivation than that of the Sigurd story.

(*PMLA*, xvii, 262–95) as *Signy's Lament*, a lyric to be related to the story of the Volsung revenge. Certain objections can be interposed to this identification of the poem as a lament of Signy, but it is somewhat generally conceded, to quote Bradley, that 'the imagined speaker is a lady whose circumstances closely resemble the e of Signy.'

55. ll.884–98.

THE FINNSBURG LAY

We have no means of checking the *Finnsburg Episode* of the *Beowulf* by historical record. And yet, so vivid is the story, and so typically Germanic the dramatic situations set forth, that the story of Finnsburg reads like tribal tradition realistically rooted in tragic event. In addition to the passage in the *Beowulf,* we have, fortunately, one other record of the Finnsburg story, a fragment of 48 lines, defective at beginning and end.[56] The action of the *Finnsburg Fragment* precedes the action of the *Beowulf Episode* and, in spite of difficulties of detail, the relation of the *Fragment* to the *Episode* can be reconstructed with reasonable clearness.

Neither the *Episode* nor the *Fragment* throws any light upon the origin of the feud between Danes and Frisians which had such tragic denouement at Finnsburg. But we find in the *Episode* a not unfamiliar Teutonic situation. Hildeburh, daughter of Hoc of the Half-Danes, was married to Finn, the Frisian king. It is possible that she had been wedded to Finn in order to compose the Frisian feud, as Hrothgar purposed to compose the Heathobard feud by the marriage of Freawaru to Ingeld. If so, the feud was of long standing, since Hildeburh had a son old enough to die in battle. If Hildeburh's office was that of 'peace-weaver' she was doomed to as tragic a failure as Beowulf prophesied for the diplomatic marriage of Freawaru.

Whatever the origin and early history of the feud, at the time indicated in the *Fragment* we find a company of Danes under their king, Hnæf, visiting the Frisian king, Finn, in

56. The manuscript of this fragment was discovered by Hickes in the library of Lambeth Palace. It was transcribed by him, and printed in his *Thesaurus.* Unfortunately, the manuscript has since been lost, and the text today rests solely on Hickes' transcription.

his stronghold at Finnsburg. One night just before daybreak Hnæf and sixty retainers were attacked in hall by a band of Finn's men. A warrior on guard reported flashes and gleams of light outside the hall, but was uncertain of the cause. Were the gables of the hall on fire? Was it a fire-breathing dragon flying through the night? Was it the glimmer of daybreak? Hnæf recognized the light as the gleam of moonlight on weapons and armor. It is an attack on the hall! The *Fragment* begins with Hnæf's spirited call to arms:

> This is not dawn, nor flying dragon,
> Nor fire burning the horns of this hall,
> But men in armor! The eagle will scream,
> The gray wolf howl, and the war-wood whistle,
> Shield answer shaft! Now shines the moon
> Through scudding cloud. Dire deeds are come
> Bringing hard battle and bitter strife.
> Awake my warriors! Grasp your shields!
> Fight like men in the front of battle!
> Be bold of mood; be mindful of glory!

The Danes rushed to defend the doors, Sigeferth and Eaha guarding one door; Ordlaf, Guthlaf, and Hengest, the other. Garulf, the leader of the attacking band, shouted his challenge, asking who guarded the door. 'Sigeferth! lord of the Secgan,' was the answer; 'I have known much hardship and many bitter battles. From me you can get what you are looking for!' Then din of battle rose; bucklers broke and hallboards resounded. Garulf was the first to fall, and many a good man lay stretched beside him. 'Swords flashed as if all Finnsburg were on fire.' 'I have never heard,' the poet says of the Danes, 'of sixty heroes who made better requital for the shining mead than his warriors made to Hnæf!' For five days they fought, and not one fell, and they held the doors. Then one of Finn's men, with armor battered and broken, turned away from the battle. His lord inquired of him how the wounded men were holding out, and which of the men —and at this point the *Fragment* breaks off.

How much time elapsed between the events of the *Fragment* and the events of the *Episode* has been a matter of discussion. When the *Fragment* breaks off, Hnæf and his sixty warriors are still alive. They had held the doors for five days, and not one had fallen. But more and more of Finn's men must have been drawn into the battle until losses became heavy on both sides. At last, we learn from the *Episode,* Hnæf fell in the slaughter, and on the Frisian side Hnæf's nephew, Hildeburh's son, was slain.

Exhausted by the indecisive struggle, with many dead on both sides, Hengest and the surviving Danes made a truce with Finn. Under its terms the Danes accepted the overlordship of Finn, and in turn were to receive a hall of their own, and equal justice and honor with the people of Finn. If any should reproach Hengest or his men with following the slayer of their lord, or in any manner awaken the old feud, punishment by the sword would be the penalty.

There follows in the *Episode* a realistic description of the burning of the dead. A great funeral pyre was constructed, and on it, side by side, were placed the bodies of Hnæf and his nephew. Beside the pyre, Hildeburh lamented the fall of her kinsmen.

The greatest of funeral fires
Rolled with a roar to the skies at the burial barrow.
Heads melted and gashes gaped, the mortal wounds of
   the body;

Blood poured out in the flames; the fire, most greedy
   of spirits,
Swallowed up all whom battle had taken of both
   their peoples.

During the long months that followed, when 'winter
locked ocean with bonds of ice,' Hengest and his men were
forced to remain at Finnsburg. But the Danes were unhappy
under the truce. Guthlaf and Oslaf could not bridle their
restive spirits. And Hengest's thoughts 'were more of re-
venge than of voyaging over the wave.' When the sunny,
shining days of Spring returned, a son of Hunlaf one day
laid in Hengest's lap a naked battle-sword whose edge was
already well known to the men of Finn, a hint that loyalty
required vengeance for the death of Hnæf. Once more the
feud broke out; the hall ran red with blood. Finn was killed,
and Hildeburh, with much treasure, was taken back to Den-
mark to her own people.

Although the course of events at Finnsburg can be visual-
ized along these general lines, it must be recognized that
there are many elements of uncertainty in the tale, and ques-
tions which cannot be answered from the text. We do not
know what considerations caused the visit of the Danes to
Finnsburg. We do not know whether the attack upon the
hall in the *Fragment* represents the outbreak of hostilities, or
whether the peace had already been broken by the Danes
themselves. We cannot be certain of all the details of the
truce sworn to by Finn and Hengest. And, perhaps most per-
plexing of all, we cannot be completely certain as to the part
played at Finnsburg by the Jutes. They are mentioned four
times in the course of the *Episode*,[57] and the various interpre-

57. ll.1072, 1088, 1141, 1145.

tations of these references represent divergent theories as to elements of motivation in the stream of tragic event. Judgment on these points requires a detailed consideration not possible here. The reader who desires to pursue the tempting and tantalizing vistas which the Finnsburg story opens to us should consult the enlightening studies of *Episode* and *Fragment* by Lawrence, Chambers, and Williams.[58]

CHRISTIAN INFLUENCE

We have seen that the primitive material of the *Beowulf* was derived from pagan folk-tale, chronicle, and legend, and slowly welded into new unities. It remained for the Old English poet to complete this process of fusion by the conversion, or transmutation, of this material from pagan to Christian. The epic emerges at last as a Christian poem. This mutation, moreover, is not merely a matter of altered phrases, or of interpolated references to the Christian faith, but is a deeply pervasive infusion of Christian spirit coloring thought and judgment, governing motive and action, a continuous and active agent in the process of transformation.

This mutation of material could not, in the nature of things, be absolute or complete. There are pagan elements in

58. Lawrence ('Beowulf and the Tragedy of Finnsburg,' *PMLA*, xxx, 372-431 and *Beowulf and Epic Tradition*, 107-28) regards the allusions to the Jutes and Frisians as interchangeable references to Finn's men. From this he derives an interpretation of extreme tragic conflict between Hengest's loyalty to Hnæf, his dead leader, and the oath to Finn, which circumstances force him to undertake. Chambers (*Beowulf, An Introduction,* 245-89) differentiates the Jutes from the Frisians, exculpating Finn of guilt in the attack on Hnæf, and justifying Hengest's oath to Finn as compatible with the obligations of the blood feud. R.A.Williams (*The Finn Episode in Beowulf*, Cambridge, 1924) in an ingenious examination of the Finnsburg problems differs at points from both Lawrence and Chambers. His reconstruction of the Finn saga brings this material into comparison with the story of the Burgundians in the second part of the *Nibelungenlied*. As to the validity of the use of *Nibelungenlied* material to guide reconstruction of the Finn story, see Chambers (*Beowulf, An Introduction*, 284, note).

the poem that resist change, or that are only partially sub-
dued by the influence of the Christian spirit. The presence
in the poem of references to the curse upon the dragon's
hoard is one example, of many, of the persistence of pagan
tradition in a Christian poem. Other examples of this in-
complete fusion of pagan and Christian will be found in a
parallelism of reference to the blind and inexorable power of
Wyrd, or Fate, and to the omnipotence of a divine Ruler
who governs all things well. But even in survivals of pagan
material the modifying influence of Christian thought is
often evident. In both instances in which there is reference
to the curse upon the dragon's treasure[59] the poet specifically
excludes from the operation of the curse one who has God's
favor. Elsewhere in the poem, *God* and *Wyrd* are brought
into juxtaposition in such manner as to imply control of Fate
by the superior power of Christian divinity. The original
derivation of Grendel and his dam from the Scandinavian
waterfall troll is submerged and lost in the poet's identi-
fication of the monsters with the fiends of Christian myth-
ology, incarnations of evil, and adversaries of God. Though
Beowulf has a remote prototype in the laggard younger son
of folk-tale and has been accorded a place in the succession
of Geatish kings, his character has been recast and developed
in the spirit of the Christian tradition. Throughout the poem
divine guidance is invoked, and acknowledged, as the assist-
ing force by which the heroic deeds of Beowulf are accom-
plished. After his death his fame is celebrated not only, and
not most, for valor and venturous deeds, but for the gentler
qualities of Christian virtue. And it is precisely this presence
in the poem of pagan derivatives modified by Christian in-
fluence, which points, in Chambers' opinion, to the Age of

59. ll.3052, 3069.

Bede, rather than a later date, as the period in which the *Beowulf* was written.[60]

The Christian influence in the *Beowulf* is a matter of transforming spirit, rather than of reference to dogma or doctrine. And it is, in the main, an influence reflecting the Old Testament rather than the New. The poem contains specific references to Cain's murder of Abel, and to the stories of the Creation, the giants, and the Flood. But we find no such allusions to New Testament themes as characterize, for example, the *Christ* of Cynewulf. Indeed, considering the nature of the material with which the poet is working, we should hardly expect such references.

Some critics have believed that the *Beowulf* was composed not by a Christian, but by a pagan poet, and that the presence of the Christian material is to be explained by subsequent excision of pagan, and interpolation of Christian, passages. Others have argued that the Christian elements represent the work of a poet with only vague and general knowledge of the new faith, or merely nominal adherence to it. The weight of evidence does not support such opinion. The Christian spirit is too deeply ingrained in the poem to permit the hypothesis of original composition by a pagan poet. A just appraisal of the pervasive nature of these Christian elements supports Chambers' opinion that the *Beowulf* can not be regarded as 'the work of a man whose adherence to Christianity is merely nominal.'[61]

It is not unnatural, therefore, that the essentially Christian

60. 'Bede shows us examples of Christianity as complete in their gentleness, humility, and charity as any we shall find in English history. Yet the old pagan heroic ideals were certainly still alive. The stories of the minstrelsy of Caedmon and of Aldhelm show us men quite consciously trying to harmonize the new and the old.' *Beowulf, An Introduction*, p.488.

61. *Beowulf, An Introduction*, p.126.

genius of the poem is most clearly perceived, not so much in
details of Biblical theme and phrasing, as in those passages in
which Christian ethics are central in shaping speech and in-
fluencing conduct. We find such a passage in the homiletic
speech of Hrothgar in which the Danish king paints for
Beowulf a warning portrait of the man betrayed by worldly
prosperity into pride, and by pride into sin:

> He lives in luxury, knowing not want,
> Knowing no shadow of sickness or age;
> No haunting sorrow darkens his spirit,
> No hatred or discord deepens to war;
> The world is sweet, to his every desire,
> And evil assails not—until in his heart
> Pride overpowering gathers and grows!
> The warden slumbers, the guard of his spirit;
> Too sound is that sleep, too sluggish the weight
> Of worldly affairs, too pressing the Foe,
> The Archer who looses the arrows of sin.[62]

The substance and import of this *exemplum* are clearly in
the tradition of the medieval Christian moralist. The treat-
ment of the material affords an unusually interesting illustra-
tion of the manner in which the Christian spirit is at work in
the poem, transforming and supplementing the stuff of pagan
tradition. The similarity of this passage to the material and
spirit of certain passages in Cynewulf's *Christ* and *Juliana* has
often been noted. But the eighty-five lines of Hrothgar's
speech[63] have seemed to some critics an inartistic interrup-
tion of the narrative, tediously homiletic in substance. Such
a judgment seems to overlook, or underestimate, the process

62. ll.1735-44.
63. ll.1700-84.

by which a cruder system of pagan morals is being reshaped in these lines by the criteria of Christian ethics.

It must be recognized that Hrothgar's warning against the sin of pride, and its corroding effect in character, is by no means an unnatural intrusion into the narrative. To understand fully the spirit of his advice to the young Beowulf, we must remember the closeness of the tie that had grown up between them. It is not only a natural gratitude for deeds of knight-errantry that motivates Hrothgar's words, but also a warm personal affection. He has already adopted Beowulf as a foster son,[64] and at their final parting there are tears in the old king's eyes and grief in his foreboding that they may never meet again.[65] It is, therefore, not unnatural that in these last hours he should muster, from ripe old age and experience, words of kindly counsel to the youth whose heroic career is now in its brilliant dawn. And it is not unnatural that the Christian poet should give the turn to the passage which he does give.

The warning example which Hrothgar uses is the career of Heremod. The wrongs for which the name of Heremod was execrated were the evils of violence and greed in his relations with his *comitatus* and with his people. He slew his followers in fits of drunken rage, and failed in the generous bestowal of rewards which the *comitatus* relation required from lord to retainer. He was unfaithful to the two outstanding obligations imposed by the *comitatus* bond, the duty to protect and to reward his followers. These obligations were rooted in a pagan institution, and infringements were censurable under a pagan code. Censure and warning in this

64. ll.946-9.
65. ll.1871-6.

passage, therefore, could have been grounded on purely pagan convention.

But the Christian poet, in his homily on pride, derives from the story of Heremod ethical judgments that go beyond the pagan code. He traces the sins of violence and greed backward to roots in pride, and forward to punishment here and hereafter. The concepts of a pagan morality are expanded into Christian ethics in a formal passage suggestive of the moralizing allegories of virtue and vice so characteristic of later medieval literature.

When all is said, the fact remains, since the *Beowulf* is not a religious but a secular poem, that its Christian elements are more general and diffused than is characteristic of distinctively religious Old English poetry. The old heroic themes furnish stubborn material, and retain some portion of their native strength even in the hands of a Christian poet. The nature and degree of the Christian influence is best understood when one estimates the poem as a composite of traditional themes of pagan heroism retold by a Christian poet. The resulting fusion of pagan and Christian is what could naturally be expected under such circumstances. The material affords no opportunity for reflections of the intimate and personal responses of the individual soul to the Christian drama of the New Testament. We need not look for mystical adoration as in the *Dream of the Rood,* or for echoes of the liturgy as in *Christ I,* or for reflections of theological dogma as in *Christ II.* The *Beowulf* is a tale of the pagan past in which the endurance, the loyalty, the courage, and the strength of the heroic age are tempered by union with Christian virtues, graced with courtly manners, and elevated in presentment to levels of epic dignity.

THE INFLUENCE OF CLASSICAL EPIC

It is difficult to estimate precisely the degree of influence
exerted by classical epic, particularly the *Aeneid,* upon the
shaping of the *Beowulf.* It would certainly not be unnatural
that we should find reflections of the Virgilian epic in the
form and spirit of the Old English poem. The *Aeneid* was
well known in the early Middle Ages. We have record that
Bede, Aldhelm, and Alcuin were lovers of Virgil, and it
would seem unlikely that an educated poet of the Age of
Bede could have shaped the epic tale of Beowulf without
having had in mind the model of the classical epic. Careful
study of the two poems has shown that there are many lines
in the *Beowulf* which read like echoes of Virgilian phrase,
and elements of structure which suggest parallels in the
Aeneid. Klaeber, in an article entitled 'Aeneis und Beowulf,'[66]
and Haber, in his comparative study of the *Beowulf* and the
Aeneid,[67] have compiled exhaustive lists of parallelisms in
phrase, theme, and situation.

It seems unlikely that additional parallels between the
Beowulf and the *Aeneid* remain to be discovered. But there
is a possible influence of the *Aeneid* upon a passage in the
Old English poem which has not hitherto been pointed out.
A description in the *Beowulf* of Grendel's mere, a finely
wrought passage of twenty lines (1357–76), lingers in the
mind of many a reader as perhaps the finest 'set-piece' of the
poem. The descriptive suggestiveness of this picture of the
forbidding landscape of Grendel's pool affords evidence of a

66. *Archiv für das Studium der neueren Sprachen und Literaturen,* cxxvi, 40-8;
339-59.

67. *A Comparative Study of the Beowulf and the Aeneid,* Princeton University
Press, 1931.

sensitively poetic mind at work. The passage is a familiar one, and has received extended consideration by many critics. As long ago as 1912, in a study entitled 'The Haunted Mere in Beowulf,'[68] Lawrence gave us an admirable analysis of this passage, and an illuminating comparison with corresponding material in the *Grettissaga*.

At three points in the *Beowulf* passage, parallelisms to seemingly correspondent, or at least suggestive, passages in the *Aeneid* have been listed.[69] In each of the three instances, the *Beowulf* text has several suggested parallels in the *Aeneid,* and, perhaps for this reason, it has not been emphasized that *one* possible parallel for *each* of the three passages in the *Beowulf* is found within a scope of 92 lines (479–571) in the Seventh Book of the *Aeneid.* If the Old English poet, then, had recently been reading the Seventh Book he might from this reading have had lodged in memory three elements which have been unified in his description of Grendel's mere: the hart pursued by hounds, the stormy waves that rise to the sky, the gloomy landscape of the mountain torrent. This fact is significant and suggestive, presenting, as it does, the possibility that fused reminiscence of elements from a comparatively short passage of Virgil influenced the development of Hrothgar's famous description of Grendel's pool.

The possibility of such fused reminiscence in these lines of the *Beowulf* seems no less likely for the fact that in the Virgilian passage[70] the three elements cited are not unified, as they are in the *Beowulf,* as elements in a single passage of description. The reference to the stormy waves rising to the

68. *PMLA*, xxvii, 208–45.

69. *Beowulf* 1357–67 to *Aeneid* vi, 136–9; 237·8, 295–7, 369, 438; vii, 565–71; xi, 522–5. *Beowulf* 1368–72 to *Aeneid* iv, 69–73; vii, 479–504; xii, 749–55. *Beowulf* 1373–5 to *Aeneid* i, 133–4; iii, 422–3; v, 790–1; vii, 529–30; xii, 204–5.

70. *Aeneid*, vii, 479–571.

sky occurs in the *Aeneid* as the material of a Virgilian simile. The episode of the hunted stag is introduced as a motivation in the design of the Fury, Allecto, to stir up war between the Latins and the Trojans. The painting of a forbidding landscape occurs in a description of the Vale of Amsanctus, a hell-mouth, into which, her purpose fulfilled, Allecto sank, and 'relieved earth and heaven of her hateful presence.'

The parallelism I have cited deserves special consideration, both because of the triple nature of the resemblance involved, and because of the bearing of the Virgilian passage upon a statement in Hrothgar's description, the appropriateness of which in its context is at least dubious. If we think of the poet as shaping his inherited material with realism, and uninfluenced by literary reminiscence, lines 1373–6 of the *Beowulf* seem inappropriate in a description of an inland lake, or pool, or swamp. If it is an inland mere that we are dealing with, and the weight of evidence seems to indicate that it *is* inland water, and not an arm of the sea, then it is difficult for the reader to accept even a poetic statement that 'from it the tossing waves rise dark to the sky, when the wind stirs up foul weather.' Such a statement is surely far more applicable to the high waves on a storm-tossed ocean, and this is undoubtedly the reference in Virgil's simile.[71] But if we postulate that the Old English poet, dealing with a landscape not wholly understood, is composing description less realistic than literary, and with a vivid sea simile of the *Aeneid* in memory, the possibility of Virgilian coloring in these lines of the *Beowulf* becomes clearer.

71. Fluctus uti primo coepit cum albescere vento,
     Paulatim sese tollit mare, et altius undas
     Erigit, inde imo consurgit ad aethera fundo.
                    Aeneid VII, 528–30.

The possibility that Virgil's description of the Vale of Amsanctus[72] is reflected in lines 1359-64 of Hrothgar's description seems also to deserve close attention. In the Virgilian landscape a swift torrent, in swirling eddies, pours down over rocks, shut in between wooded ridges dark with foliage. There is also a 'ghastly pool,' a 'breathing-hole of the grim lord of hell, and vast chasm breaking into Acheron.' Through this hell-mouth the Fury, Allecto, returns to the underworld. Even the briefest comparison of the two passages will indicate the similarities in the two descriptions: the mountain torrents, the ridges or cliffs in the gloom of which these streams pour down, the trees that overshadow, the dismal and gloomy nature of the landscape.

It is interesting to remember in this connection the assertion of the *Beowulf* poet,[73] when the wounded and fleeing Grendel plunged into the mere, that there 'hell received him.' We have in this line a natural implication of the tradition by which, throughout the poem, Grendel is repeatedly identified as a demon and an enemy of God. The statement represents a foreshadowing of his death and the return of his spirit to hell. But there is a suggestiveness in the fact that in Virgil's lines the Fury, Allecto, returns to the underworld through the hell-mouth of Amsanctus.

72. Est locus Italiae medio sub montibus altis,
   Nobilis et fama multis memoratus in oris,
   Ampsancti valles; densis hunc frondibus atrum
   Urguet utrimque latus memoris, medioque fragosus
   Dat sonitum saxis et torto vertice torrens.
   Hic specus horrendum et saevi spiracula Ditis
   Monstrantur, ruptoque ingens Acheronte vorago
   Pestiferas aperit fauces: quis condita Erinys,
   Invisum numen, terras caelumque levabat.
                                    Aeneid VII, 563-71.

73. l.852.

Virgil's wounded stag of the Seventh Book[74] has no such role as the *Beowulf* poet assigns his antlered hart in suggesting the eerie nature of the mere by willingness to die upon the bank rather than enter the water. But again it is significant that Virgil's stag is upon the bank of a stream, and turns away from it when wounded and pursued by hounds. The reasons in the two instances are quite different, but the situations are the same in this respect, that in each poem we have a stag wounded, pursued by hounds, and at the water's edge, and in each instance the stag turns away from the water to die.

The attempt to appraise the influence of one work upon another is properly approached with caution. Critics most convinced of the influence of the *Aeneid* upon the *Beowulf* may be least convinced of the validity of particular parallels. And we must not forget that the Old English poet had inherited a scenery original with his folk-tale material, however it may have been modified in tradition. But it would in no way be unnatural if his reshaping of this inherited material had been influenced by details from Virgil which could so easily fuse with the scenic elements of his original. If any single passage of the *Beowulf* tempts one to believe that the Old English poet was composing with pen guided by reminiscence of the *Aeneid,* it is, I think, this description of Grendel's mere and the hints of Virgil's Seventh Book that seem latent in it.

74. Cervus erat forma praestanti et cornibus ingens,
   Tyrrhidae pueri quem matris ab ubere raptum
   Nutribant, Tyrrheusque pater, cui regia parent
   Armenta, et late custodia credita campi . . .
   Hunc procul errantem rabidae venantis Iuli
   Commovere canes, fluvio cum forte secundo
   Deflueret, ripaque aestus viridante levaret.
   Aeneid VII, 483-6, 493-5.

In any attempt to isolate and appraise an influence of the *Aeneid* upon the *Beowulf*, we meet with difficulties. The manners and customs of the Age of Troy were in many ways like the manners and customs of the Germanic Heroic Age, representing similar cultural levels and similar folk-ways. Parallels between the two poems, then, may arise from similar methods in the reflection of similar conventions. It could hardly be considered surprising if the descriptions, in the two poems, of social ceremonial, of war and council, feast and funeral, should follow very similar patterns. Lists of parallels, therefore, however imposing, have not produced unqualified conviction that the *Beowulf* reveals borrowing from the *Aeneid*. Lawrence expresses the cautious opinion that 'while the influence of Vergil may be regarded as entirely possible, it cannot be conclusively established.'[75]

Judgment as to direct borrowing from the *Aeneid* does not, however, completely dispose of the question of Virgilian influence in the *Beowulf*. Even if it were granted that in all the parallelisms that exist between the two poems there is no conclusive evidence that the English poet borrowed from the Latin epic, there still remains a question as to indirect and diffused influence of the form and spirit of classical epic upon the shaping of the Old English poem. Chambers' remark on this point is important and suggestive. 'But the influence may have been none the less effective for being indirect: nor is it quite certain that the author, had he known his Virgil, would necessarily have left traces of direct borrowing. For the deep Christian feeling, which has given to *Beowulf* its almost prudish propriety and its edifying tone, is manifested by no direct and dogmatic reference to Christian personages

75. *Beowulf and Epic Tradition*, p.285.

or doctrines.'[76] It is notable that the *Beowulf*, in general form and movement, displays a literary quality of richly developed theme, and an epic dignity of speech and action, which could hardly have been completely derived from the Scandinavian heroic tale. And it is precisely this general element in the poem that could easily and naturally have come from the influence of Virgil's epic, in years in which the *Aeneid* was well known among the scholars of England.

THE SPIRIT OF THE POEM

To what extent is the *Beowulf* an old tale retold merely for the joy of the telling? To what extent is it developed as an exemplification of noble kinghood and the Christian ideal? An epic tale lends itself gracefully to purposes of doctrine, as the tradition of the epic so richly shows. A well-known letter of Edmund Spenser, outlining the design and structure of the *Faerie Queen,* sets forth in clear terms the underlying purpose with which the author had shaped the allegory of his immortal poem: 'The generall end therefore of all the booke, is to fashion a gentleman or noble person in vertuous and gentle discipline.'

It is never a simple matter to separate, in a work of art, didactic purpose from the aesthetic aims of creative imagination. And, in the case of the *Beowulf,* we have no such statement of purpose as Spenser's to throw light upon the poem, and no knowledge of the poet's identity, or way of life, by which to guide interpretation of his underlying intent. Many would define his purpose quite simply, as the desire to tell in verse an old tale of heroism, and to tell it well.

Yet many passages in the poem suggest that the author had more in mind than the mere retelling, however well, of a

76. *Beowulf, An Introduction*, pp.330-31.

heroic tale. There is a difference between stories of heroism and a narrative of a heroic life, and in the tale of *Beowulf* the reader is made to feel that the author is conscious of this difference. The Old English Christian poet, as we have seen, had his moralizing strain, and, like his Renaissance successor, may have felt that a narrative of a heroic king, elevated to epic dignity and illumined by the Christian ideal, could well serve for the fashioning of men to magnanimous and noble living.

Certain it is that under the pen of the *Beowulf* poet the stubborn stuff of Scandinavian legend is tempered and refined, and there emerges the figure of a noble and Christian king. The poem reflects the spirit, not of Scandinavia, but of English life of the seventh and early eighth centuries, presenting a blending of old folkways with new, a welding of pagan heroism with Christian virtue. The miracle of the *Beowulf* is the artistry of its refashioning. However widely the poem may range through the tribal lands of Scandinavia, the mood and spirit are the mood and spirit of England; the poetic ideal is the Christian ideal The pagan backgrounds of the poem sink into shadow. The old dark tales of men and lands beyond the sea echo as from a vast distance. The story of Beowulf becomes an English poem. It becomes a poem suited to a Christian court, and fitted for the shaping of men in 'vertuous and gentle discipline.' Even an ancient tale of pagan heroism, transformed by Christian spirit, could become an element in the stream of influence that flowed from the Christian Church. Lives of saints and martyrs formed a literature for the stirring of men's souls to faith and virtue, and side by side with such spiritual heroisms, the ancient tale of Beowulf's struggle with monster and dragon may well have lent itself to the uses of Christian allegory.

The unmistakable English strain in the *Beowulf* is perhaps clearest in the elegiac tone and moral temper of the poem. The elegiac element, which twice wells up with a poignancy suggestive of the lyric sadness of the *Wanderer* and the *Ruin,* is the poetic symbol of English life amid the scattered and ruined reminders of the Roman settlement. And in the moral temper of the poem there is clear reflection of the birth and shaping, largely through the dawning influence of the Christian faith, of nobler concepts of human relations and political duty. Feud and treachery, murder of kindred and usurpation have illustration in the poem, it is true, as they had illustration in contemporary English annals. But a new order of life is symbolized in the condemnation which, in the poem, is unfailingly directed against such manifestations of violence and crime.

The youthful Beowulf of the beginning and the aged king of the final scenes alike illustrate the chivalry of spirit that ennobles heroism. The Beowulf of the Grendel adventure was in essentials a knight-errant of his age. It was no call of duty that urged him across the sea to stake his life against monsters. Indeed, though his personal followers urged him on, Hygelac had endeavored to dissuade him from the undertaking. So we learn from his uncle's words at the banquet after Beowulf's return:

> I had no faith in this far sea-venture
> For one so beloved. Long I implored
> That you go not against the murderous monster,
> But let the South-Danes settle the feud
> Themselves with Grendel.

Such were the words of expediency! It can be granted that the poet portrays a youthful hero fired with love of adventure. But there is more than love of adventure that urges Beowulf on; there are demons to kill, and a curse to be lifted. More than once his words to Hrothgar reflect the sober spirit of one who strives with the powers of evil: 'I will fight to the death, foe against foe; then let the one whom death takes put his trust in the Judgment of God.' In all the young lad does, and says, there is courage. But, more important, there is also magnanimity.

It is in Beowulf's exercise of the powers and responsibilities of kingship that the poet stresses the hero's magnanimity and the Christian ideal. In his early manhood, refusing power for himself, Beowulf served as Protector of the young king Heardred. Becoming king at Heardred's death, he had for fifty years ruled wisely and well. At the end, as he lay dying, his thoughts were of the needs of his people. For himself, as he looked back upon his life, he rejoiced that after death the Lord of mankind could not charge against him the killing of kinsmen. His reign had been a reign of peace and justice. Abiding by his appointed lot, he had sworn no unrighteous oaths, had kept his own well, had courted no quarrels. As the smoke of his funeral pyre rose to the sky, his people lamented the passing of the kindest of earthly kings, the mildest and most gentle.

The tradition of doom in the dragon fight is a survival from the pagan world. But it has taken on new depth of implication. The tragic glory of the conflict is its illustration of man's heroic war with powers of darkness and evil beyond his strength. The tragic glory of Beowulf's death is its illustration of that fated courage which fights to the utmost, knowing the utmost will not wholly avail, yet fighting on.

The *Beowulf* is a priceless heritage from the earliest age of English poetry. Forgotten for centuries and rediscovered, it has at last, by the devotion of many scholars, come into its own, unfolding before us its ancient excellence. Across the centuries from the England of Bede it proclaims the ideal of gentleness united to strength, and valor ennobled by virtue. It speaks to the modern world in moving accents, of honor, of courage, and of faith. It is a tale of a vanishing age retold in the dawn of a new day. The pagan gods were fading into the darkness; new light was upon the world. The flash and thunder of Thor were not wholly forgotten; but the bolt was spent, and the echoes dying. The old legends of violence and blood formed shadowy background for a tale of Christian courage and virtue. Twice in a heroic lifetime mortal valor was pitted in crucial conflict with the ravening forces of evil. Twice a hero turned back the invading dark. In his youth he conquered and lived; in age, he conquered and died. To live or to die was as fate might ordain. To conquer was all.

BEOWULF

*The line numbering at the foot of each page
is based upon the Klaeber text.*

﹡§[*The Danish Court and the Raids of Grendel*]

Lo! we have listened to many a lay
Of the Spear-Danes' fame, their splendor of old,
Their mighty princes, and martial deeds!
Many a mead-hall Scyld, son of Sceaf,
Snatched from the forces of savage foes.
From a friendless foundling, feeble and wretched,
He grew to a terror as time brought change.
He throve under heaven in power and pride
Till alien peoples beyond the ocean
Paid toll and tribute. A good king he!

To him thereafter an heir was born,
A son of his house, whom God had given
As stay to the people; God saw the distress
The leaderless nation had long endured.
The Giver of glory, the Lord of life,
Showered fame on the son of Scyld;
His name was honored, Beowulf known,
To the farthest dwellings in Danish lands.
So must a young man strive for good
With gracious gifts from his father's store,
That in later seasons, if war shall scourge,
A willing people may serve him well.
'Tis by earning honor a man must rise
In every state. Then his hour struck,
And Scyld passed on to the peace of God.

As their leader had bidden, whose word was law
In the Scylding realm which he long had ruled,

[1-30]

His loving comrades carried him down
To the shore of ocean; a ring-prowed ship,
Straining at anchor and sheeted with ice,
Rode in the harbor, a prince's pride.
Therein they laid him, their well-loved lord,
Their ring-bestower, in the ship's embrace,
The mighty prince at the foot of the mast
Amid much treasure and many a gem
From far-off lands. No lordlier ship
Have I ever heard of, with weapons heaped,
With battle-armor, with bills and byrnies.
On the ruler's breast lay a royal treasure
As the ship put out on the unknown deep.
With no less adornment they dressed him round,
Or gift of treasure, than once they gave
Who launched him first on the lonely sea
While still but a child. A golden standard
They raised above him, high over head,
Let the wave take him on trackless seas.
Mournful their mood and heavy their hearts;
Nor wise man nor warrior knows for a truth
Unto what haven that cargo came.

     Then Beowulf ruled o'er the Scylding realm,
Beloved and famous, for many a year—
The prince, his father, had passed away—
Till, firm in wisdom and fierce in war,
The mighty Healfdene held the reign,
Ruled, while he lived, the lordly Scyldings.
Four sons and daughters were seed of his line,
Heorogar and Hrothgar, leaders of hosts,
And Halga, the good. I have also heard

[30–62]

A daughter was Onela's consort and queen,
The fair bed-mate of the Battle-Scylfing.

  To Hrothgar was granted glory in war,
Success in battle; retainers bold
Obeyed him gladly; his band increased
To a mighty host. Then his mind was moved
To have men fashion a high-built hall,
A mightier mead-hall than man had known,
Wherein to portion to old and young
All goodly treasure that God had given,
Save only the folk-land, and lives of men.
His word was published to many a people
Far and wide o'er the ways of earth
To rear a folk-stead richly adorned;
The task was speeded, the time soon came
That the famous mead-hall was finished and done.
To distant nations its name was known,
The Hall of the Hart; and the king kept well
His pledge and promise to deal out gifts,
Rings at the banquet. The great hall rose
High and horn-gabled, holding its place
Till the battle-surge of consuming flame
Should swallow it up; the hour was near
That the deadly hate of a daughter's husband
Should kindle to fury and savage feud.

  Then an evil spirit who dwelt in the darkness
Endured it ill that he heard each day
The din of revelry ring through the hall,
The sound of the harp, and the scop's sweet song.
A skillful bard sang the ancient story
Of man's creation; how the Maker wrought

[62-92]

The shining earth with its circling waters;
In splendor established the sun and moon
As lights to illumine the land of men;
Fairly adorning the fields of earth
With leaves and branches; creating life
In every creature that breathes and moves.
So the lordly warriors lived in gladness,
At ease and happy, till a fiend from hell
Began a series of savage crimes.
They called him Grendel, a demon grim
Haunting the fen-lands, holding the moors,
Ranging the wastes, where the wretched wight
Made his lair with the monster kin;
He bore the curse of the seed of Cain
Whereby God punished the grievous guilt
Of Abel's murder. Nor ever had Cain
Cause to boast of that deed of blood;
God banished him far from the fields of men;
Of his blood was begotten an evil brood,
Marauding monsters and menacing trolls,
Goblins and giants who battled with God
A long time. Grimly He gave them reward!
Then at the nightfall the fiend drew near
Where the timbered mead-hall towered on high,
To spy how the Danes fared after the feast.
Within the wine-hall he found the warriors
Fast in slumber, forgetting grief,
Forgetting the woe of the world of men.
Grim and greedy the gruesome monster,
Fierce and furious, launched attack,
Slew thirty spearmen asleep in the hall,

[93-123]

Sped away gloating, gripping the spoil,
Dragging the dead men home to his den.
Then in the dawn with the coming of daybreak
The war-might of Grendel was widely known.
Mirth was stilled by the sound of weeping;
The wail of the mourner awoke with day.
And the peerless hero, the honored prince,
Weighed down with woe and heavy of heart,
Sat sorely grieving for slaughtered thanes,
As they traced the track of the cursed monster.
From that day onward the deadly feud
Was a long-enduring and loathsome strife.

      Not longer was it than one night later
The fiend returning renewed attack
With heart firm-fixed in the hateful war,
Feeling no rue for the grievous wrong.
'Twas easy thereafter to mark the men
Who sought their slumber elsewhere afar,
Found beds in the bowers, since Grendel's hate
Was so baldly blazoned in baleful signs.
He held himself at a safer distance
Who escaped the clutch of the demon's claw.
So Grendel raided and ravaged the realm,
One against all, in an evil war
Till the best of buildings was empty and still.
'Twas a weary while! Twelve winters' time
The lord of the Scyldings had suffered woe,
Sore affliction and deep distress.
And the malice of Grendel, in mournful lays,
Was widely sung by the sons of men,
The hateful feud that he fought with Hrothgar—

Year after year of struggle and strife,
An endless scourging, a scorning of peace
With any man of the Danish might.
No strength could move him to stay his hand,
Or pay for his murders; the wise knew well
They could hope for no halting of savage assault.
Like a dark death-shadow the ravaging demon,
Night-long prowling the misty moors,
Ensnared the warriors, wary or weak.
No man can say how these shades of hell
Come and go on their grisly rounds.

     With many an outrage, many a crime,
The fierce lone-goer, the foe of man,
Stained the seats of the high-built house,
Haunting the hall in the hateful dark.
But throne or treasure he might not touch,
Finding no favor or grace with God.
Great was the grief of the Scylding leader,
His spirit shaken, while many a lord
Gathered in council considering long
In what way brave men best could struggle
Against these terrors of sudden attack.
From time to time in their heathen temples
Paying homage they offered prayer
That the Slayer of souls would send them succor
From all the torment that troubled the folk.
Such was the fashion and such the faith
Of their heathen hearts that they looked to hell,
Not knowing the Maker, the mighty Judge,
Nor how to worship the Wielder of glory,
The Lord of heaven, the God of hosts.

[153-183]

Woe unto him who in fierce affliction
Shall plunge his soul in the fiery pit
With no hope of mercy or healing change;
But well with the soul that at death seeks God,
And finds his peace in his Father's bosom.

    The son of Healfdene was heavy-hearted,
Sorrowfully brooding in sore distress,
Finding no help in a hopeless strife;
Too bitter the struggle that stunned the people,
The long oppression, loathsome and grim.

⌇[*The Coming of Beowulf*]

    Then tales of the terrible deeds of Grendel
Reached Hygelac's thane in his home with the Geats;
Of living strong men he was the strongest,
Fearless and gallant and great of heart.
He gave command for a goodly vessel
Fitted and furnished; he fain would sail
Over the swan-road to seek the king
Who suffered so sorely for need of men.
And his bold retainers found little to blame
In his daring venture, dear though he was;
They viewed the omens, and urged him on.
Brave was the band he had gathered about him,
Fourteen stalwarts seasoned and bold,
Seeking the shore where the ship lay waiting,
A sea-skilled mariner sighting the landmarks.
Came the hour of boarding; the boat was riding
The waves of the harbor under the hill.
The eager mariners mounted the prow;
Billows were breaking, sea against sand.

[183–213]

In the ship's hold snugly they stowed their trappings,
Gleaming armor and battle-gear;
Launched the vessel, the well-braced bark,
Seaward bound on a joyous journey.
Over breaking billows, with bellying sail
And foamy beak, like a flying bird
The ship sped on, till the next day's sun
Showed sea-cliffs shining, towering hills
And stretching headlands. The sea was crossed,
The voyage ended, the vessel moored.
And the Weder people waded ashore
With clatter of trappings and coats of mail;
Gave thanks to God that His grace had granted
Sea-paths safe for their ocean-journey.
    Then the Scylding coast-guard watched from the
      sea-cliff
Warriors bearing their shining shields,
Their gleaming war-gear, ashore from the ship.
His mind was puzzled, he wondered much
What men they were. On his good horse mounted,
Hrothgar's thane made haste to the beach,
Boldly brandished his mighty spear
With manful challenge: 'What men are you,
Carrying weapons and clad in steel,
Who thus come driving across the deep
On the ocean-lanes in your lofty ship?
Long have I served as the Scylding outpost,
Held watch and ward at the ocean's edge
Lest foreign foemen with hostile fleet
Should come to harry our Danish home,
And never more openly sailed to these shores

[213-245]

Men without password, or leave to land.
I have never laid eyes upon earl on earth
More stalwart and sturdy than one of your troop,
A hero in armor; no hall-thane he
Tricked out with weapons, unless looks belie him,
And noble bearing. But now I must know
Your birth and breeding, nor may you come
In cunning stealth upon Danish soil.
You distant-dwellers, you far sea-farers,
Hearken, and ponder words that are plain:
'Tis best you hasten to have me know
Who your kindred and whence you come.'
    The lord of the seamen gave swift reply,
The prince of the Weders unlocked his word-hoard:
'We are sprung of a strain of the Geatish stock,
Hygelac's comrades and hearth-companions.
My father was famous in many a folk-land,
A leader noble, Ecgtheow his name!
Many a winter went over his head
Before death took him from home and tribe;
Well nigh every wise man remembers him well
Far and wide on the ways of earth.
With loyal purpose we seek your lord,
The prince of your people, great Healfdene's son.
Be kindly of counsel; weighty the cause
That leads us to visit the lord of the Danes;
Nor need it be secret, as far as I know!
You know if it's true, as we've heard it told,
That among the Scyldings some secret scather,
Some stealthy demon in dead of night,
With grisly horror and fiendish hate

[245-276]

Is spreading unheard-of havoc and death.
Mayhap I can counsel the good, old king
What way he can master the merciless fiend,
If his coil of evil is ever to end
And feverish care grow cooler and fade—
Or else ever after his doom shall be
Distress and sorrow while still there stands
This best of halls on its lofty height.'
    Then from the saddle the coast-guard spoke,
The fearless sentry: 'A seasoned warrior
Must know the difference between words and deeds,
If his wits are with him. I take your word
That your band is loyal to the lord of the Scyldings.
Now go your way with your weapons and armor,
And I will guide you; I'll give command
That my good retainers may guard your ship,
Your fresh-tarred floater, from every foe,
And hold it safe in its sandy berth,
Till the curving prow once again shall carry
The loved man home to the land of the Geat.
To hero so gallant shall surely be granted
To come from the swordplay sound and safe.'
    Then the Geats marched on; behind at her mooring,
Fastened at anchor, their broad-beamed boat
Safely rode on her swinging cable.
Boar-heads glittered on glistening helmets
Above their cheek-guards, gleaming with gold;
Bright and fire-hardened the boar held watch
Over the column of marching men.
Onward they hurried in eager haste
Till their eyes caught sight of the high-built hall,

[276-308]

Splendid with gold, the seat of the king,
Most stately of structures under the sun;
Its light shone out over many a land.
The coast-guard showed them the shining hall,
The home of heroes; made plain the path;
Turned his horse; gave tongue to words:
'It is time to leave you! The mighty Lord
In His mercy shield you and hold you safe
In your bold adventure. I'll back to the sea
And hold my watch against hostile horde.'

✑§ [Beowulf's Welcome at Hrothgar's Court]

The street had paving of colored stone;
The path was plain to the marching men.
Bright were their byrnies, hard and hand-linked;
In their shining armor the chain-mail sang
As the troop in their war-gear tramped to the hall.
The sea-weary sailors set down their shields,
Their wide, bright bucklers along the wall,
And sank to the bench. Their byrnies rang.
Their stout spears stood in a stack together
Shod with iron and shaped of ash.
'Twas a well-armed troop! Then a stately warrior
Questioned the strangers about their kin:
'Whence come you bearing your burnished shields,
Your steel-gray harness and visored helms,
Your heap of spears? I am Hrothgar's herald,
His servant-thane. I have never seen strangers,
So great a number, of nobler mien.
Not exiles, I ween, but high-minded heroes
In greatness of heart have you sought out Hrothgar.'

[308–339]

Then bold under helmet the hero made answer,
The lord of the Weders, manful of mood,
Mighty of heart: 'We are Hygelac's men,
His board-companions; Beowulf is my name.
I will state my mission to Healfdene's son,
The noble leader, your lordly prince,
If he will grant approach to his gracious presence.'
And Wulfgar answered, the Wendel prince,
Renowned for merit in many a land,
For war-might and wisdom: 'I will learn the wish
Of the Scylding leader, the lord of the Danes,
Our honored ruler and giver of rings,
Concerning your mission, and soon report
The answer our leader thinks good to give.'
    He swiftly strode to where Hrothgar sat
Old and gray with his earls about him;
Crossed the floor and stood face to face
With the Danish king; he knew courtly custom.
Wulfgar saluted his lord and friend:
'Men from afar have fared to our land
Over ocean's margin—men of the Geats,
Their leader called Beowulf—seeking a boon,
The holding of parley, my prince, with thee.
O gracious Hrothgar, refuse not the favor!
In their splendid war-gear they merit well
The esteem of earls; he's a stalwart leader
Who led this troop to the land of the Danes.'
    Hrothgar spoke, the lord of the Scyldings:
'Their leader I knew when he still was a lad.
His father was Ecgtheow; Hrethel the Geat
Gave him in wedlock his only daughter.

[340-375]

Now is their son come, keen for adventure,
Finding his way to a faithful friend.
Sea-faring men who have voyaged to Geatland
With gifts of treasure as token of peace,
Say that his hand-grip has thirty men's strength.
God, in His mercy, has sent him to save us—
So springs my hope—from Grendel's assaults.
For his gallant courage I'll load him with gifts!
Make haste now, marshal the men to the hall,
And give them welcome to Danish ground.'
    Then to the door went the well-known warrior,
Spoke from the threshold welcoming words:
'The Danish leader, my lord, declares
That he knows your kinship; right welcome you come,
You stout sea-rovers, to Danish soil.
Enter now, in your shining armor
And vizored helmets, to Hrothgar's hall.
But leave your shields and the shafts of slaughter
To wait the issue and weighing of words.'
    Then the bold one rose with his band around him,
A splendid massing of mighty thanes;
A few stood guard as the Geat gave bidding
Over the weapons stacked by the wall.
They followed in haste on the heels of their leader
Under Heorot's roof. Full ready and bold
The helmeted warrior strode to the hearth;
Beowulf spoke; his byrny glittered,
His war-net woven by cunning of smith:
'Hail! King Hrothgar! I am Hygelac's thane,
Hygelac's kinsman. Many a deed
Of honor and daring I've done in my youth.

[375-409]

This business of Grendel was brought to my ears
On my native soil. The sea-farers say
This best of buildings, this boasted hall,
Stands dark and deserted when sun is set,
When darkening shadows gather with dusk.
The best of my people, prudent and brave,
Urged me, King Hrothgar, to seek you out;
They had in remembrance my courage and might.
Many had seen me come safe from the conflict,
Bloody from battle; five foes I bound
Of the giant kindred, and crushed their clan.
Hard-driven in danger and darkness of night
I slew the nicors that swam the sea,
Avenged the woe they had caused the Weders,
And ended their evil—they needed the lesson!
And now with Grendel, the fearful fiend,
Single-handed I'll settle the strife!
Prince of the Danes, protector of Scyldings,
Lord of nations, and leader of men,
I beg one favor—refuse me not,
Since I come thus faring from far-off lands—
That I may alone with my loyal earls,
With this hardy company, cleanse Hart-Hall.
I have heard that the demon in proud disdain
Spurns all weapons; and I too scorn—
May Hygelac's heart have joy of the deed—
To bear my sword, or sheltering shield,
Or yellow buckler, to battle the fiend.
With hand-grip only I'll grapple with Grendel;
Foe against foe I'll fight to the death,
And the one who is taken must trust to God's grace!

[409-441]

The demon, I doubt not, is minded to feast
In the hall unaffrighted, as often before,
On the force of the Hrethmen, the folk of the Geats.
No need then to bury the body he mangles!
If death shall call me, he'll carry away
My gory flesh to his fen-retreat
To gorge at leisure and gulp me down,
Soiling the marshes with stains of blood.
There'll be little need longer to care for my body!
If the battle slays me, to Hygelac send
This best of corselets that covers my breast,
Heirloom of Hrethel, and Wayland's work,
Finest of byrnies. Fate goes as Fate must!'
    Hrothgar spoke, the lord of the Scyldings:
'Deed of daring and dream of honor
Bring you, friend Beowulf, knowing our need!
Your father once fought the greatest of feuds,
Laid Heatholaf low, of the Wylfing line;
And the folk of the Weders refused him shelter
For fear of revenge. Then he fled to the South-Danes,
The Honor-Scyldings beyond the sea.
I was then first governing Danish ground,
As a young lad ruling the spacious realm,
The home-land of warriors. Heorogar was dead,
The son of Healfdene no longer living,
My older brother, and better than I!
Thereafter by payment composing the feud,
O'er the water's ridge I sent to the Wylfing
Ancient treasure; he swore me oaths!
It is sorrow sore to recite to another
The wrongs that Grendel has wrought in the hall,

[442-475]

His savage hatred and sudden assaults.
My war-troop is weakened, my hall-band is wasted;
Fate swept them away into Grendel's grip.
But God may easily bring to an end
The ruinous deeds of the ravaging foe.
Full often my warriors over their ale-cups
Boldly boasted, when drunk with beer,
They would bide in the beer-hall the coming of battle,
The fury of Grendel, with flashing swords.
Then in the dawn, when the daylight strengthened,
The hall stood reddened and reeking with gore,
Bench-boards wet with the blood of battle;
And I had the fewer of faithful fighters,
Beloved retainers, whom Death had taken.
Sit now at the banquet, unbend your mood,
Speak of great deeds as your heart may spur you!'
    Then in the beer-hall were benches made ready
For the Geatish heroes. Noble of heart,
Proud and stalwart, they sat them down
And a beer-thane served them; bore in his hands
The patterned ale-cup, pouring the mead,
While the scop's sweet singing was heard in the hall.
There was joy of heroes, a host at ease,
A welcome meeting of Weder and Dane.

◦§[Unferth Taunts Beowulf]

    Then out spoke Unferth, Ecglaf's son,
Who sat at the feet of the Scylding lord,
Picking a quarrel—for Beowulf's quest,
His bold sea-voyaging, irked him sore;
He bore it ill that any man other

[476-503]

In all the earth should ever achieve
More fame under heaven than he himself:
'Are you the Beowulf that strove with Breca
In a swimming match in the open sea,
Both of you wantonly tempting the waves,
Risking your lives on the lonely deep
For a silly boast? No man could dissuade you,
Nor friend nor foe, from the foolhardy venture
Of ocean-swimming; with outstretched arms
You clasped the sea-stream, measured her streets,
With plowing shoulders parted the waves.
The sea-flood boiled with its wintry surges,
Seven nights you toiled in the tossing sea;
His strength was the greater, his swimming the stronger!
The waves upbore you at break of day
To the stretching beach of the Battle-Ræmas;
And Breca departed, beloved of his people,
To the land of the Brondings, the beauteous home,
The stronghold fair, where he governed the folk,
The city and treasure; Beanstan's son
Made good his boast to the full against you!
Therefore, I ween, worse fate shall befall,
Stout as you are in the struggle of war,
In deeds of battle, if you dare to abide
Encounter with Grendel at coming of night.'
    Beowulf spoke, the son of Ecgtheow:
'My good friend Unferth, addled with beer
Much have you made of the deeds of Breca!
I count it true that I had more courage,
More strength in swimming than any other man.
In our youth we boasted—we were both of us boys—

[504-537]

We would risk our lives in the raging sea.
And we made it good! We gripped in our hands
Naked swords, as we swam in the waves,
Guarding us well from the whales' assault.
In the breaking seas he could not outstrip me,
Nor would I leave him. For five nights long
Side by side we strove in the waters
Till racing combers wrenched us apart,
Freezing squalls, and the falling night,
And a bitter north wind's icy blast.
Rough were the waves; the wrath of the sea-fish
Was fiercely roused; but my firm-linked byrny,
The gold-adorned corselet that covered my breast,
Gave firm defense from the clutching foe.
Down to the bottom a savage sea-beast
Fiercely dragged me and held me fast
In a deadly grip; none the less it was granted me
To pierce the monster with point of steel.
Death swept it away with the swing of my sword.
        The grisly sea-beasts again and again
Beset me sore; but I served them home
With my faithful blade as was well-befitting.
They failed of their pleasure to feast their fill
Crowding round my corpse on the ocean-bottom!
Bloody with wounds, at the break of day,
They lay on the sea-beach slain with the sword.
No more would they cumber the mariner's course
On the ocean deep. From the east came the sun,
Bright beacon of God, and the seas subsided;
I beheld the headlands, the windy walls.
Fate often delivers an undoomed earl

[537-573]

If his spirit be gallant! And so I was granted
To slay with the sword-edge nine of the nicors.
I have never heard tell of more terrible strife
Under dome of heaven in darkness of night,
Nor of man harder pressed on the paths of ocean.
But I freed my life from the grip of the foe
Though spent with the struggle. The billows bore me,
The swirling currents and surging seas,
To the land of the Finns. And little I've heard
Of any such valiant adventures from you!
Neither Breca nor you in the press of battle
Ever showed such daring with dripping swords—
Though I boast not of it! But you stained your blade
With blood of your brothers, your closest of kin;
And for that you'll endure damnation in hell,
Sharp as you are! I say for a truth,
Son of Ecglaf, never had Grendel
Wrought such havoc and woe in the hall,
That horrid demon so harried your king,
If your heart were as brave as you'd have men think!
But Grendel has found that he never need fear
Revenge from your people, or valiant attack
From the Victor-Scyldings; he takes his toll,
Sparing none of the Danish stock.
He slays and slaughters and works his will
Fearing no hurt at the hands of the Danes!
But soon will I show him the stuff of the Geats,
Their courage in battle and strength in the strife;
Then let him who may go bold to the mead-hall
When the next day dawns on the dwellings of men,
And the sun in splendor shines warm from the south.'

[573-606]

Glad of heart was the giver of treasure,
Hoary-headed and hardy in war;
The lordly leader had hope of help
As he listened to Beowulf's bold resolve.

      There was revel of heroes and high carouse,
Their speech was happy; and Hrothgar's queen,
Of gentle manners, in jewelled splendor
Gave courtly greeting to all the guests.
The high-born lady first bore the beaker
To the Danish leader, lord of the land,
Bade him be blithe at the drinking of beer;
Beloved of his people, the peerless king
Joined in the feasting, had joy of the cup.
Then to all alike went the Helming lady
Bearing the beaker to old and young,
Till the jewelled queen with courtly grace
Paused before Beowulf, proffered the mead.
She greeted the Geat and to God gave thanks,
Wise of word, that her wish was granted;
At last she could look to a hero for help,
Comfort in evil. He took the cup,
The hardy warrior, at Wealhtheow's hand
And, eager for battle, uttered his boast;
Beowulf spoke, the son of Ecgtheow:
'I had firm resolve when I set to sea
With my band of earls in my ocean-ship,
Fully to work the will of your people
Or fall in the struggle slain by the foe.
I shall either perform deeds fitting an earl
Or meet in this mead-hall the coming of death!'
Then the woman was pleased with the words he uttered,

[607–639]

The Geat-lord's boast; the gold-decked queen
Went in state to sit by her lord.

৯§[*Beowulf Slays Grendel*]

In the hall as of old were brave words spoken,
There was noise of revel; happy the host
Till the son of Healfdene would go to his rest.
He knew that the monster would meet in the hall
Relentless struggle when light of the sun
Was dusky with gloom of the gathering night,
And shadow-shapes crept in the covering dark,
Dim under heaven. The host arose.
Hrothgar graciously greeted his guest,
Gave rule of the wine-hall, and wished him well,
Praised the warrior in parting words:
'Never to any man, early or late,
Since first I could brandish buckler and sword,
Have I trusted this ale-hall save only to you!
Be mindful of glory, show forth your strength,
Keep watch against foe! No wish of your heart
Shall go unfulfilled if you live through the fight.'
        Then Hrothgar withdrew with his host of retainers,
The prince of the Scyldings, seeking his queen,
The bed of his consort. The King of Glory
Had stablished a hall-watch, a guard against Grendel,
Dutifully serving the Danish lord,
The land defending from loathsome fiend.
The Geatish hero put all his hope
In his fearless might and the mercy of God!
He stripped from his shoulders the byrny of steel,
Doffed helmet from head; into hand of thane

[640–673]

Gave inlaid iron, the best of blades;
Bade him keep well the weapons of war.
Beowulf uttered a gallant boast,
The stalwart Geat, ere he sought his bed:
'I count myself nowise weaker in war
Or grapple of battle than Grendel himself.
Therefore I scorn to slay him with sword,
Deal deadly wound, as I well might do!
Nothing he knows of a noble fighting,
Of thrusting and hewing and hacking of shield,
Fierce as he is in the fury of war.
In the shades of darkness we'll spurn the sword
If he dares without weapon to do or to die.
And God in His wisdom shall glory assign,
The ruling Lord, as He deems it right.'
Then the bold in battle bowed down to his rest,
Cheek pressed pillow; the peerless thanes
Were stretched in slumber around their lord.
Not one had hope of return to his home,
To the stronghold or land where he lived as a boy.
For they knew how death had befallen the Danes,
How many were slain as they slept in the wine-hall.
But the wise Lord wove them fortune in war,
Gave strong support to the Weder people;
They slew their foe by the single strength
Of a hero's courage. The truth is clear,
God rules forever the race of men.
        Then through the shades of enshrouding night
The fiend came stealing; the archers slept
Whose duty was holding the horn-decked hall—
Though one was watching—full well they knew

[673-705]

No evil demon could drag them down
To shades under ground if God were not willing.
But the hero watched awaiting the foe,
Abiding in anger the issue of war.

From the stretching moors, from the misty hollows,
Grendel came creeping, accursed of God,
A murderous ravager minded to snare
Spoil of heroes in high-built hall.
Under clouded heavens he held his way
Till there rose before him the high-roofed house,
Wine-hall of warriors gleaming with gold.
Nor was it the first of his fierce assaults
On the home of Hrothgar; but never before
Had he found worse fate or hardier hall-thanes!
Storming the building he burst the portal,
Though fastened of iron, with fiendish strength;
Forced open the entrance in savage fury
And rushed in rage o'er the shining floor.
A baleful glare from his eyes was gleaming
Most like to a flame. He found in the hall
Many a warrior sealed in slumber,
A host of kinsmen. His heart rejoiced;
The savage monster was minded to sever
Lives from bodies ere break of day,
To feast his fill of the flesh of men.
But he was not fated to glut his greed
With more of mankind when the night was ended!

The hardy kinsman of Hygelac waited
To see how the monster would make his attack.
The demon delayed not, but quickly clutched
A sleeping thane in his swift assault,

[706-741]

Tore him in pieces, bit through the bones,
Gulped the blood, and gobbled the flesh,
Greedily gorged on the lifeless corpse,
The hands and the feet. Then the fiend stepped nearer,
Sprang on the Sea-Geat lying outstretched,
Clasping him close with his monstrous claw.
But Beowulf grappled and gripped him hard,
Struggled up on his elbow; the shepherd of sins
Soon found that never before had he felt
In any man other in all the earth
A mightier hand-grip; his mood was humbled,
His courage fled; but he found no escape!
He was fain to be gone; he would flee to the darkness,
The fellowship of devils. Far different his fate
From that which befell him in former days!
The hardy hero, Hygelac's kinsman,
Remembered the boast he had made at the banquet;
He sprang to his feet, clutched Grendel fast,
Though fingers were cracking, the fiend pulling free.
The earl pressed after; the monster was minded
To win his freedom and flee to the fens.
He knew that his fingers were fast in the grip
Of a savage foe. Sorry the venture,
The raid that the ravager made on the hall.

There was din in Heorot. For all the Danes,
The city-dwellers, the stalwart Scyldings,
That was a bitter spilling of beer!
The walls resounded, the fight was fierce,
Savage the strife as the warriors struggled.
The wonder was that the lofty wine-hall
Withstood the struggle, nor crashed to earth,

[741-772]

The house so fair; it was firmly fastened
Within and without with iron bands
Cunningly smithied; though men have said
That many a mead-bench gleaming with gold
Sprang from its sill as the warriors strove.
The Scylding wise men had never weened
That any ravage could wreck the building,
Firmly fashioned and finished with bone,
Or any cunning compass its fall,
Till the time when the swelter and surge of fire
Should swallow it up in a swirl of flame.

    Continuous tumult filled the hall;
A terror fell on the Danish folk
As they heard through the wall the horrible wailing,
The groans of Grendel, the foe of God
Howling his hideous hymn of pain,
The hell-thane shrieking in sore defeat.
He was fast in the grip of the man who was greatest
Of mortal men in the strength of his might,
Who would never rest while the wretch was living,
Counting his life-days a menace to man.

    Many an earl of Beowulf brandished
His ancient iron to guard his lord,
To shelter sately the peerless prince.
They had no knowledge, those daring thanes,
When they drew their weapons to hack and hew,
To thrust to the heart, that the sharpest sword,
The choicest iron in all the world,
Could work no harm to the hideous foe.
On every sword he had laid a spell,
On every blade; but a bitter death

[773–805]

Was to be his fate; far was the journey
The monster made to the home of fiends.

Then he who had wrought such wrong to men,
With grim delight as he warred with God,
Soon found that his strength was feeble and failing
In the crushing hold of Hygelac's thane.
Each loathed the other while life should last!
There Grendel suffered a grievous hurt,
A wound in the shoulder, gaping and wide;
Sinews snapped and bone-joints broke,
And Beowulf gained the glory of battle.
Grendel, fated, fled to the fens,
To his joyless dwelling, sick unto death.
He knew in his heart that his hours were numbered,
His days at an end. For all the Danes
Their wish was fulfilled in the fall of Grendel.
The stranger from far, the stalwart and strong,
Had purged of evil the hall of Hrothgar,
And cleansed of crime; the heart of the hero
Joyed in the deed his daring had done.
The lord of the Geats made good to the East-Danes
The boast he had uttered; he ended their ill,
And all the sorrow they suffered long'
And needs must suffer—a foul offense.
The token was clear when the bold in battle
Laid down the shoulder and dripping claw—
Grendel's arm—in the gabled hall!

&[*The Joy of the Danes and the Lay of Sigemund*]

When morning came, as they tell the tale,
Many a warrior hastened to hall,

[806-838]

Folk-leaders faring from far and near
Over wide-running ways, to gaze at the wonder,
The trail of the demon. Nor seemed his death
A matter of sorrow to any man
Who viewed the tracks of the vanquished monster
As he slunk weary-hearted away from the hall,
Doomed and defeated and marking his flight
With bloody prints to the nicors' pool.
The crimson currents bubbled and heaved
In eddying reaches reddened with gore;
The surges boiled with the fiery blood.
But the monster had sunk from the sight of men.
In that fenny covert the cursed fiend
Not long thereafter laid down his life,
His heathen spirit; and hell received him.
　　　Then all the comrades, the old and young,
The brave of heart, in a blithesome band
Came riding their horses home from the mere.
Beowulf's prowess was praised in song;
And many men stated that south or north,
Over all the world, or between the seas,
Or under the heaven, no hero was greater,
More worthy of rule. But no whit they slighted
The gracious Hrothgar, their good old king.
Time and again they galloped their horses,
Racing their roans where the roads seemed fairest;
Time and again a gleeman chanted,
A minstrel mindful of saga and lay.
He wove his words in a winsome pattern,
Hymning the burden of Beowulf's feat,
Clothing the story in skillful verse.

[839–874]

All tales he had ever heard told he sang of Sigemund's glory,
Deeds of the Wælsing forgotten, his weary roving and wars,
Feuds and fighting unknown to men, save Fitela only,
Tales told by uncle to nephew when the two were companions,
What time they were bosom-comrades in battle and bitter strife.
Many of monster blood these two had slain with the sword-edge;
Great glory Sigemund gained that lingered long after death,
When he daringly slew the dragon that guarded the hoard of gold.
Under the ancient rock the warrior ventured alone,
No Fitela fighting beside him; but still it befell
That his firm steel pierced the worm, the point stood fast in the
    wall;
The dragon had died the death! And the hero's daring
Had won the treasure to have and to hold as his heart might wish.
Then the Wælsing loaded his sea-boat, laid in the breast of the
    ship
Wondrous and shining treasure; the worm dissolved in the heat.
Sigemund was strongest of men in his deeds of daring,
Warrior's shield and defender, most famous in days of old
After Heremod's might diminished, his valor and vigor in war,
Betrayed in the land of the Jutes to the hands of his foemen, and
    slain.
Too long the surges of sorrow swept over his soul; in the end
His life was a lingering woe to people and princes.
In former days his fate was mourned by many a warrior
Who had trusted his lord for protection from terror and woe,
Had hoped that the prince would prosper, wielding his father's
    wealth,
Ruling the tribe and the treasure, the Scylding city and home.
Hygelac's kinsman had favor and friendship of all mankind,
But the stain of sin sank deep into Heremod's heart.

[874–915]

Time and again on their galloping steeds
Over yellow roads they measured the mile-paths;
Morning sun mounted the shining sky
And many a hero strode to the hall,
Stout of heart, to behold the wonder.
The worthy ruler, the warder of treasure,
Set out from the bowers with stately train;
The queen with her maidens paced over the mead-path.
Then spoke Hrothgar; hasting to hall
He stood at the steps, stared up at the roof
High and gold-gleaming; saw Grendel's hand:
'Thanks be to God for this glorious sight!
I have suffered much evil, much outrage from Grendel,
But the God of glory works wonder on wonder.
I had no hope of a haven from sorrow
While this best of houses stood badged with blood,
A woe far-reaching for all the wise
Who weened that they never could hold the hall
Against the assaults of devils and demons.
But now with God's help this hero has compassed
A deed our cunning could no way contrive.
Surely that woman may say with truth,
Who bore this son, if she still be living,
Our ancient God showed favor and grace
On her bringing-forth! O best of men,
I will keep you, Beowulf, close to my heart
In firm affection; as son to father
Hold fast henceforth to this foster-kinship.
You shall know not want of treasure or wealth
Or goodly gift that your wish may crave,
While I have power. For poorer deeds

[916–951]

I have granted guerdon, and graced with honor
Weaker warriors, feebler in fight.
You have done such deeds that your fame shall flourish
Through all the ages! God grant you still
All goodly grace as He gave before.'
      Beowulf spoke, the son of Ecgtheow:
'By the favor of God we won the fight,
Did the deed of valor, and boldly dared
The might of the monster. I would you could see
The fiend himself lying dead before you!
I thought to grip him in stubborn grasp
And bind him down on the bed of death,
There to lie straining in struggle for life,
While I gripped him fast lest he vanish away.
But I might not hold him or hinder his going
For God did not grant it, my fingers failed.
Too savage the strain of his fiendish strength!
To save his life he left shoulder and claw,
The arm of the monster, to mark his track.
But he bought no comfort; no whit thereby
Shall the wretched ravager racked with sin,
The loathsome spoiler, prolong his life.
A deep wound holds him in deadly grip,
In baleful bondage; and black with crime
The demon shall wait for the day of doom
When the God of glory shall give decree.'
      Then slower of speech was the son of Ecglaf,
More wary of boasting of warlike deeds,
While the nobles gazed at the grisly claw,
The fiend's hand fastened by hero's might
On the lofty roof. Most like to steel

[951-985]

Were the hardened nails, the heathen's hand-spurs,
Horrible, monstrous; and many men said
No tempered sword, no excellent iron,
Could have harmed the monster or hacked away
The demon's battle-claw dripping with blood.

ᴥᴥ[*The Feast and the Lay of Finnsburg*]

In joyful haste was Heorot decked
And a willing host of women and men
Gaily dressed and adorned the guest-hall.
Splendid hangings with sheen of gold
Shone on the walls, a glorious sight
To eyes that delight to behold such wonders.
The shining building was wholly shatered
Though braced and fastened with iron bands;
Hinges were riven; the roof alone
Remained unharmed when the horrid monster,
Foul with evil, slunk off in flight,
Hopeless of life. It is hard to flee
The touch of death, let him try who will;
Necessity urges the sons of men,
The dwellers on earth, to their destined place
Where the body, bound in its narrow bed,
After the feasting is fast in slumber.

Soon was the time when the son of Healfdene
Went to the wine-hall; he fain would join
With happy heart in the joy of feasting.
I never have heard of a mightier muster
Of proud retainers around their prince.
All at ease they bent to the benches,
Had joy of the banquet; their kinsmen bold,

[985-1014]

Hrothgar and Hrothulf, happy of heart,
In the high-built hall drank many a mead-cup.
The hall of Hrothgar was filled with friends;
No treachery yet had troubled the Scyldings.
Upon Beowulf, then, as a token of triumph,
Hrothgar bestowed a standard of gold,
A banner embroidered, a byrny and helm.
In sight of many, a costly sword
Before the hero was borne on high;
Beowulf drank of many a bowl.
No need for shame in the sight of heroes
For gifts so gracious! I never have heard
Of many men dealing in friendlier fashion,
To others on ale-bench, richer rewards,
Four such treasures fretted with gold!
On the crest of the helmet a crowning wreath,
Woven of wire-work, warded the head
Lest tempered swordblade, sharp from the file,
Deal deadly wound when the shielded warrior
Went forth to battle against the foe.
Eight horses also with plated headstalls
The lord of heroes bade lead into hall;
On one was a saddle skillfully fashioned
And set with jewels, the battle-seat
Of the king himself, when the son of Healfdene
Would fain take part in the play of swords;
Never in fray had his valor failed,
His kingly courage, when corpses were falling.
And the prince of the Ingwines gave all these gifts
To the hand of Beowulf, horses and armor;
Bade him enjoy them! With generous heart

[1014-1046]

The noble leader, the lord of heroes,
Rewarded the struggle with steeds and with treasure,
So that none can belittle, and none can blame,
Who tells the tale as it truly happened.

    Then on the ale-bench to each of the earls
Who embarked with Beowulf, sailing the sea-paths,
The lord of princes dealt ancient heirlooms,
Gift of treasure, and guerdon of gold
To requite his slaughter whom Grendel slew,
As he would have slain others, but all-wise God
And the hero's courage had conquered Fate.
The Lord ruled over the lives of men
As He rules them still. Therefore understanding
And a prudent spirit are surely best!
He must suffer much of both weal and woe
Who dwells here long in these days of strife.

    Then song and revelry rose in the hall;
Before Healfdene's leader the harp was struck
And hall-joy wakened; the song was sung,
Hrothgar's gleeman rehearsed the lay
Of the sons of Finn when the terror befell them:

    *Hnæf of the Scyldings, the Half-Dane, fell in the Frisian
slaughter;*
Nor had Hildeburh cause to acclaim the faith of the Jutish folk,
Blameless, bereft of her brothers in battle, and stripped of her sons
Who fell overcome by their fate and wounded with spears!
Not for nothing Hoc's daughter bewailed death's bitter decree,
In the dawn under morning skies, when she saw the slaughter of
  kinsmen

[1046-1079]

*In the place where her days had been filled with the fairest delights
   of the world.
Finn's thanes were slain in the fight, save only a few;
Nor could he do battle with Hengest or harry his shattered host;
And the Frisians made terms with the Danes, a truce, a hall for
   their dwelling,
A throne, and a sharing of rights with the sons of the Jutes,
And that Finn, the son of Folcwalda, each day would honor the
   Danes,
The host of Hengest, with gifts, with rings and guerdon of gold,
Such portion of plated treasure as he dealt to the Frisian folk
When he gladdened their hearts in the hall. So both were bound by
   the truce.
And Finn swore Hengest with oaths that were forceful and firm
He would rightfully rule his remnant, follow his council's decree,
And that no man should break the truce, or breach it by word or
   by will,
Nor the lordless in malice lament they were fated to follow
The man who had murdered their liege; and, if ever a Frisian
Fanned the feud with insolent speech, the sword should avenge it.
      Then a funeral pyre was prepared, and gold was drawn from
   the hoard,
The best of the Scylding leaders was laid on the bier;
In the burning pile was a gleaming of blood-stained byrnies,
The gilded swine and the boar-helm hard from the hammer,
Many a warrior fated with wounds and fallen in battle.
And Hildeburh bade that her son be laid on the bier of Hnæf,
His body consumed in the surging flame at his uncle's shoulder.
Beside it the lady lamented, singing her mournful dirge.
The hero was placed on the pyre; the greatest of funeral flames
Rolled with a roar to the skies at the burial barrow.*

[1079–1120]

Heads melted and gashes gaped, the mortal wounds of the body,
Blood poured out in the flames; the fire, most greedy of spirits,
Swallowed up all whom battle had taken of both their peoples.
Their glory was gone! The warriors went to their homes,
Bereft of their friends, returning to Friesland, to city and strong-
   hold.
     Then Hengest abode with Finn all the slaughter-stained
   winter,
But his heart longed ever for home, though he could not launch
   on the sea
His ring-stemmed ship, for the billows boiled with the storm,
Strove with the wind, and the winter locked ocean in bonds of ice;
Till a new Spring shone once more on the dwellings of men,
The sunny and shining days which ever observe their season.
The winter was banished afar, and fair the bosom of earth.
Then the exile longed to be gone, the guest from his dwelling,
But his thoughts were more on revenge than on voyaging over the
   wave,
Plotting assault on the Jutes, renewal of war with the sword.
So he spurned not the naked hint when Hunlafing laid in his lap
The battle-flasher, the best of blades, well known to the Jutes!
In his own home death by the sword befell Finn, the fierce-hearted,
When Guthlaf and Oslaf requited the grim attack,
The woe encountered beyond the sea, the sorrow they suffered,
Nor could bridle the restive spirits within their breasts!
     Then the hall was reddened with blood and bodies of foemen,
Finn killed in the midst of his men, and the fair queen taken.
The Scylding warriors bore to their ships all treasure and wealth,
Such store as they found in the home of Finn of jewels and gems.
And the noble queen they carried across the sea-paths,
Brought her back to the Danes, to her own dear people.

[1120–1159]

So the song was sung, the lay recited,
The sound of revelry rose in the hall.
Stewards poured wine from wondrous vessels;
And Wealhtheow, wearing a golden crown,
Came forth in state where the two were sitting,
Courteous comrades, uncle and nephew,
Each true to the other in ties of peace.
Unferth, the orator, sat at the feet
Of the lord of the Scyldings; and both showed trust
In his noble mind, though he had no mercy
On kinsmen in swordplay; the Scylding queen spoke:
'My sovereign lord, dispenser of treasure,
Drink now of this flagon, have joy of the feast!
Speak to the Geats, O gold-friend of men,
In winning words as is well-befitting;
Be kind to the Geat-men and mindful of gifts
From the gold you have garnered from near and far.
You have taken as son, so many have told me,
This hardy hero. Heorot is cleansed,
The gleaming gift-hall. Rejoice while you may
In lavish bounty, and leave to your kin
People and kingdom when time shall come,
Your destined hour, to look on death.
I know the heart of my gracious Hrothulf,
That he'll safely shelter and shield our sons
When you leave this world, if he still is living.
I know he will favor with gracious gifts
These boys of ours, if he bears in mind
The many honors and marks of love
We bestowed upon him while he still was a boy.'
      She turned to the bench where her boys were sitting,

[1159–1183]

Hrethric and Hrothmund, the sons of heroes,
The youth together; there the good man sat,
Beowulf of the Geats, beside the two brothers.
Then the cup was offered with gracious greeting,
And seemly presents of spiraled gold,
A corselet, and rings, and the goodliest collar
Of all that ever were known on earth.
I have never heard tell of a worthier treasure
In the hoarding of heroes beneath the sky
Since Hama bore off to the shining city
The Brosings' jewel, setting and gems,
Fled from Eormenric's cruel craft
And sought the grace of eternal glory.
Hygelac, the Geat, grandson of Swerting
Wore the ring in the last of his raids,
Guarding the spoil under banner in battle,
Defending the treasure. Overtaken by Fate,
In the flush of pride he fought with the Frisians
And met disaster. The mighty prince
Carried the ring o'er the cup of the waves,
The precious jewel, and sank under shield.
Then his body fell into Frankish hands,
His woven corselet and jewelled collar,
And weaker warriors plundered the dead
After the carnage and welter of war.
The field of battle was covered with corpses
Of Geats who had fallen, slain by the sword.
    The sound of revelry rose in the hall;
Wealhtheow spoke to the warrior host:
'Take, dear Beowulf, collar and corselet,
Wear these treasures with right good will!

[1184–1218]

Thrive and prosper and prove your might!
Befriend my boys with your kindly counsel;
I will remember and I will repay.
You have earned the undying honor of heroes
In regions reaching as far and wide
As the windy walls that the sea encircles.
May Fate show favor while life shall last!
I wish you wealth to your heart's content;
In your days of glory be good to my sons!
Here each hero is true to other,
Gentle of spirit, loyal to lord,
Friendly thanes and a folk united,
Wine-cheered warriors who do my will.'

❧ [The Troll-Wife Avenges Grendel]

Then she went to her seat. At the fairest of feasts
Men drank of the wine-cup, knowing not Fate,
Nor the fearful doom that befell the earls
When darkness gathered, and gracious Hrothgar
Sought his dwelling and sank to rest.
A host of heroes guarded the hall
As they oft had done in the days of old.
They stripped the benches and spread the floor
With beds and bolsters. But one of the beer-thanes
Bowed to his hall-rest doomed to death.
They set at their heads their shining shields,
Their battle-bucklers; and there on the bench
Above each hero his towering helmet,
His spear and corselet hung close at hand.
It was ever their wont to be ready for war
At home or in field, as it ever befell

[1218–1249]

That their lord had need. 'Twas a noble race!
      Then they sank to slumber. But one paid dear
For his evening rest, as had often happened
When Grendel haunted the lordly hall
And wrought such ruin, till his end was come,
Death for his sins; it was easily seen,
Though the monster was slain, an avenger survived
Prolonging the feud, though the fiend had perished.
The mother of Grendel, a monstrous hag,
Brooded over her misery, doomed to dwell
In evil waters and icy streams
From ancient ages when Cain had killed
His only brother, his father's son.
Banished and branded with marks of murder
Cain fled far from the joys of men,
Haunting the barrens, begetting a brood
Of grisly monsters; and Grendel was one,
The fiendish ogre who found in the hall
A hero on watch, and awaiting the fray.
The monster grappled; the Geat took thought
Of the strength of his might, that marvelous gift
Which the Lord had given; in God he trusted
For help and succor and strong support,
Whereby he humbled the fiend from hell,
Destroyed the demon; and Grendel fled,
Harrowed in heart and hateful to man,
Deprived of joy, to the place of death.
But rabid and raging his mother resolved
On a dreadful revenge for the death of her son!
      She stole to the hall where the Danes were sleeping,
And horror fell on the host of earls

[1249-1281]

When the dam of Grendel burst in the door.
But the terror was less as the war-craft is weaker,
A woman's strength, than the might of a man
When the hilted sword, well shaped by the hammer,
The blood-stained iron of tempered edge,
Hews the boar from the foeman's helmet.
Then in the hall was the hard-edged blade,
The stout steel, brandished above the benches;
Seizing their shields men stayed not for helmet
Or ample byrny, when fear befell.
As soon as discovered, the hag was in haste
To fly to the open, to flee for her life.
One of the warriors she swiftly seized,
Clutched him fast and made off to the fens.
He was of heroes the dearest to Hrothgar,
The best of comrades between two seas;
The warrior brave, the stout-hearted spearman,
She slew in his sleep. Nor was Beowulf there;
But after the banquet another abode
Had been assigned to the glorious Geat.
There was tumult in Heorot. She tore from its place
The blood-stained claw. Care was renewed!
It was no good bargain when both in turn
Must pay the price with the lives of friends!
Then the white-haired warrior, the aged king,
Was numb with sorrow, knowing his thane
No longer was living, his dearest man dead.
Beowulf, the brave, was speedily summoned,
Brought to the bower; the noble prince
Came with his comrades at dawn of day
Where the wise king awaited if God would award

[1281-1314]

Some happier turn in these tidings of woe.
The hero came tramping into the hall
With his chosen band—the boards resounded—
Greeted the leader, the Ingwine lord,
And asked if the night had been peaceful and pleasant.

    Hrothgar spoke, the lord of the Scyldings:
'Ask not of pleasure; pain is renewed
For the Danish people. Æschere is dead!
Dead is Yrmenlaf's elder brother!
He was my comrade, closest of counsellors,
My shoulder-companion as side by side
We fought for our lives in the welter of war,
In the shock of battle when boar-helms crashed.
As an earl should be, a prince without peer,
Such was Æschere, slain in the hall
By the wandering demon! I know not whither
She fled to shelter, proud of her spoil,
Gorged to the full. She avenged the feud
Wherein yesternight you grappled with Grendel
And savagely slew him because so long
He had hunted and harried the men of my folk.
He fell in the battle and paid with his life.
But now another fierce ravager rises
Avenging her kinsman, and carries it far,
As it seems to many a saddened thane
Who grieves in his heart for his treasure-giver.
This woe weighs heavy! The hand lies still
That once was lavish of all delights.

    Oft in the hall I have heard my people,
Comrades and counsellors, telling a tale
Of evil spirits their eyes have sighted,

[1315–1347]

Two mighty marauders who haunt the moors.
One shape, as clearly as men could see,
Seemed woman's likeness, and one seemed man,
An outcast wretch of another world,
And huger far than a human form.
Grendel my countrymen called him, not knowing
What monster-brood spawned him, what sire begot.
Wild and lonely the land they live in,
Wind-swept ridges and wolf-retreats,
Dread tracts of fen where the falling torrent
Downward dips into gloom and shadow
Under the dusk of the darkening cliff.
Not far in miles lies the lonely mere
Where trees firm-rooted and hung with frost
Overshroud the wave with shadowing gloom.
And there a portent appears each night,
A flame in the water; no man so wise
Who knows the bound of its bottomless depth.
The heather-stepper, the horned stag,
The antlered hart hard driven by hounds,
Invading that forest in flight from afar
Will turn at bay and die on the brink
Ere ever he'll plunge in that haunted pool.
'Tis an eerie spot! Its tossing spray
Mounts dark to heaven when high winds stir
The driving storm, and the sky is murky,
And with foul weather the heavens weep.
On your arm only rests all our hope!
Not yet have you tempted those terrible reaches
The region that shelters that sinful wight.
Go if you dare! I will give requital

[1347-1380]

With ancient treasure and twisted gold,
As I formerly gave in guerdon of battle,
If out of that combat you come alive.'
  Beowulf spoke, the son of Ecgtheow:
'Sorrow not, brave one! Better for man
To avenge a friend than much to mourn.
All men must die; let him who may
Win glory ere death. That guerdon is best
For a noble man when his name survives him.
Then let us rise up, O ward of the realm,
And haste us forth to behold the track
Of Grendel's dam. And I give you pledge
She shall not in safety escape to cover,
To earthy cavern, or forest fastness,
Or gulf of ocean, go where she may.
This day with patience endure the burden
Of every woe, as I know you will.'
Up sprang the ancient, gave thanks to God
For the heartening words the hero had spoken.

৺[Beowulf Slays the Troll-Wife]

  Quickly a horse was bridled for Hrothgar,
A mettlesome charger with braided mane;
In royal splendor the king rode forth
Mid the trampling tread of a troop of shieldmen.
The tracks lay clear where the fiend had fared
Over plain and bottom and woodland path,
Through murky moorland making her way
With the lifeless body, the best of thanes
Who of old with Hrothgar had guarded the hall.
By a narrow path the king pressed on

[1381-1408]

Through rocky upland and rugged ravine,
A lonely journey, past looming headlands,
The lair of monster and lurking troll.
Tried retainers, a trusty few,
Advanced with Hrothgar to view the ground.
Sudden they came on a dismal covert
Of trees that hung over hoary stone,
Over churning water and blood-stained wave.
Then for the Danes was the woe the deeper,
The sorrow sharper for Scylding earls,
When they first caught sight, on the rocky sea-cliff,
Of slaughtered Æschere's severed head.
The water boiled in a bloody swirling
With seething gore as the spearmen gazed.
The trumpet sounded a martial strain;
The shield-troop halted. Their eyes beheld
The swimming forms of strange sea-dragons,
Dim serpent shapes in the watery depths,
Sea-beasts sunning on headland slopes;
Snakelike monsters that oft at sunrise
On evil errands scour the sea.
Startled by tumult and trumpet's blare,
Enraged and savage, they swam away;
But one the lord of the Geats brought low,
Stripped of his sea-strength, despoiled of life,
As the bitter bow-bolt pierced his heart.
His watery-speed grew slower, and ceased,
And he floated, caught in the clutch of death.
Then they hauled him in with sharp-hooked boar-spears,
— By sheer strength grappled and dragged him ashore,
A wondrous wave-beast; and all the array

[1409–1440]

Gathered to gaze at the grisly guest.
    Beowulf donned his armor for battle,
Heeded not danger; the hand-braided byrny,
Broad of shoulder and richly bedecked,
Must stand the ordeal of the watery depths.
Well could that corselet defend the frame
Lest hostile thrust should pierce to the heart.
Or blows of battle beat down the life.
A gleaming helmet guarded his head
As he planned his plunge to the depths of the pool
Through the heaving waters—a helm adorned
With lavish inlay and lordly chains,
Ancient work of the weapon-smith
Skillfully fashioned, beset with the boar,
That no blade of battle might bite it through.
Not the least or the worst of his war-equipment
Was the sword the herald of Hrothgar loaned
In his hour of need—Hrunting its name—
An ancient heirloom, trusty and tried;
Its blade was iron, with etched design,
Tempered in blood of many a battle.
Never in fight had it failed the hand
That drew it daring the perils of war,
The rush of the foe. Not the first time then
That its edge must venture on valiant deeds.
But Ecglaf's stalwart son was unmindful
Of words he had spoken while heated with wine,
When he loaned the blade to a better swordsman.
He himself dared not hazard his life
In deeds of note in the watery depths;
And thereby he forfeited honor and fame.

[1440-1471]

[handwritten margin notes: Unferth gives sword = peace offering; Beowulf time jumps into water; swims for a day]

Not so with that other undaunted spirit
After he donned his armor for battle.
Beowulf spoke, the son of Ecgtheow:
'O gracious ruler, gold-giver to men,
As I now set forth to attempt this feat,
Great son of Healfdene, hold well in mind
The solemn pledge we plighted of old,
That if doing your service I meet my death
You will mark my fall with a father's love.
Protect my kinsmen, my trusty comrades,
If battle take me. And all the treasure
You have heaped on me bestow upon Hygelac,
Hrothgar beloved! The lord of the Geats,
The son of Hrethel, shall see the proof,
Shall know as he gazes on jewels and gold,
That I found an unsparing dispenser of bounty,
And joyed, while I lived, in his generous gifts.
Give back to Unferth the ancient blade,
The sword-edge splendid with curving scrolls,
For either with Hrunting I'll reap rich harvest
Of glorious deeds, or death shall take me.'
    After these words the prince of the Weders
Awaited no answer, but turned to the task,
Straightway plunged in the swirling pool.
Nigh unto a day he endured the depths
Ere he first had view of the vast sea-bottom.
Soon she found, who had haunted the flood,
A ravening hag, for a hundred half-years,
Greedy and grim, that a man was groping
In daring search through the sea-troll's home.
Swift she grappled and grasped the warrior

[1471-1501]

With horrid grip, but could work no harm,
No hurt to his body; the ring-locked byrny
Cloaked his life from her clutching claw;
Nor could she tear through the tempered mail
With her savage fingers. The she-wolf bore
The ring-prince down through the watery depths
To her den at the bottom; nor could Beowulf draw
His blade for battle, though brave his mood.   *Break his armor*
Many a sea-beast, strange sea-monsters,
Tasked him hard with their menacing tusks,
Broke his byrny and smote him sore.

   Then he found himself in a fearsome hall
Where water came not to work him hurt,
But the flood was stayed by the sheltering roof.
There in the glow of firelight gleaming
The hero had view of the huge sea-troll.
He swung his war-sword with all his strength,
Withheld not the blow, and the savage blade
Sang on her head its hymn of hate.
But the bold one found that the battle-flasher
Would bite no longer, nor harm her life.
The sword-edge failed at his sorest need.
Often of old with ease it had suffered
The clash of battle, cleaving the helm,
The fated warrior's woven mail.
That time was first for the treasured blade
That its glory failed in the press of the fray.
But fixed of purpose and firm of mood
Hygelac's earl was mindful of honor;
In wrath, undaunted, he dashed to earth
The jewelled sword with its scrolled design,

[1502-1532]

The blade of steel; staked all on strength,
On the might of his hand, as a man must do
Who thinks to win in the welter of battle
Enduring glory; he fears not death.
The Geat-prince joyed in the straining struggle,
Stalwart-hearted and stirred to wrath,
Gripped the shoulder of Grendel's dam
And headlong hurled the hag to the ground.
But she quickly clutched him and drew him close,
Countered the onset with savage claw.
The warrior staggered, for all his strength,
Dismayed and shaken and borne to earth.
She knelt upon him and drew her dagger,
With broad bright blade, to avenge her son,
Her only issue. But the corselet's steel
Shielded his breast and sheltered his life
Withstanding entrance of point and edge.

 Then the prince of the Geats would have gone his
  journey,
The son of Ecgtheow, under the ground;
But his sturdy breast-net, his battle-corselet,
Gave him succor, and holy God,
The Lord all-wise, awarded the mastery;
Heaven's Ruler gave right decree.

 Swift the hero sprang to his feet;
Saw mid the war-gear a stately sword,
An ancient war-brand of biting edge,
Choicest of weapons worthy and strong,
The work of giants, a warrior's joy,
So heavy no hand but his own could hold it,
Bear to battle or wield in war.

[1533-1562]

Then the Scylding warrior, savage and grim,
Seized the ring-hilt and swung the sword,
Struck with fury, despairing of life,
Thrust at the throat, broke through the bone-rings;
The stout blade stabbed through her fated flesh.
She sank in death; the sword was bloody;
The hero joyed in the work of his hand.
The gleaming radiance shimmered and shone
As the candle of heaven shines clear from the sky.
Wrathful and resolute Hygelac's thane
Surveyed the span of the spacious hall;
Grimly gripping the hilted sword
With upraised weapon he turned to the wall.
The blade had failed not the battle-prince;
A full requital he firmly planned
For all the injury Grendel had done
In numberless raids on the Danish race,
When he slew the hearth-companions of Hrothgar,
Devoured fifteen of the Danish folk
Clasped in slumber, and carried away
As many more spearmen, a hideous spoil.
All this the stout-heart had stern requited;
And there before him bereft of life
He saw the broken body of Grendel
Stilled in battle, and stretched in death,
As the struggle in Heorot smote him down.
The corpse sprang wide as he struck the blow,
The hard sword-stroke that severed the head.

    Then the tried retainers, who there with Hrothgar
Watched the face of the foaming pool,
Saw that the churning reaches were reddened,

[1563-1593]

The eddying surges stained with blood.
And the gray, old spearmen spoke of the hero,
Having no hope he would ever return
—— Crowned with triumph and cheered with spoil.
Many were sure that the savage sea-wolf
Had slain their leader. At last came noon.
The stalwart Scyldings forsook the headland;
Their proud gold-giver departed home.
But the Geats sat grieving and sick in spirit,
Stared at the water with longing eyes,
Having no hope they would ever behold
Their gracious leader and lord again.

     Then the great sword, eaten with blood of battle,
Began to soften and waste away
In iron icicles, wonder of wonders,
Melting away most like to ice
When the Father looses the fetters of frost,
Slackens the bondage that binds the wave,
Strong in power of times and seasons;
He is true God! Of the goodly treasures
From the sea-cave Beowulf took but two,
The monster's head and the precious hilt
Blazing with gems; but the blade had melted,
The sword dissolved, in the deadly heat,
The venomous blood of the fallen fiend.

[Beowulf Returns to Heorot]

     Then he who had compassed the fall of his foes
Came swimming up through the swirling surge.
Cleansed were the currents, the boundless abyss,
Where the evil monster had died the death

[1594–1622]

And looked her last on this fleeting world.
With sturdy strokes the lord of the seamen
To land came swimming, rejoiced in his spoil,
Had joy of the burden he brought from the depths.
And his mighty thanes came forward to meet him,
Gave thanks to God they were granted to see
Their well-loved leader both sound and safe.
From the stalwart hero his helmet and byrny
Were quickly loosened; the lake lay still,
Its motionless reaches reddened with blood.
Fain of heart men fared o'er the footpaths,
Measured the ways and the well-known roads.
From the sea-cliff's brim the warriors bore
The head of Grendel, with heavy toil;
Four of the stoutest, with all their strength,
Could hardly carry on swaying spear
Grendel's head to the gold-decked hall.
Swift they strode, the daring and dauntless,
Fourteen Geats, to the Hall of the Hart;
And proud in the midst of his marching men
Their leader measured the path to the mead-hall.
The hero entered, the hardy in battle,
The great in glory, to greet the king;
And Grendel's head by the hair was carried
Across the floor where the feasters drank—
A terrible sight for lord and for lady—
A gruesome vision whereon men gazed!

    Beowulf spoke, the son of Ecgtheow:
'O son of Healfdene, lord of the Scyldings!
This sea-spoil wondrous, whereon you stare,
We joyously bring you in token of triumph!

[1622–1654]

Barely with life surviving the battle,
The war under water, I wrought the deed
Weary and spent; and death had been swift
Had God not granted His sheltering strength.
My strong-edged Hrunting, stoutest of blades,
Availed me nothing. But God revealed—
Often His arm has aided the friendless—
The fairest of weapons hanging on wall,
An ancient broadsword; I seized the blade,
Slew in the struggle, as fortune availed,
The cavern-warders. But the war-brand old,
The battle-blade with its scrolled design,
Dissolved in the gush of the venomous gore;
The hilt alone I brought from the battle.
The record of ruin, and slaughter of Danes,
These wrongs I avenged, as was fitting and right.
Now I can promise you, prince of the Scyldings,
Henceforth in Heorot rest without rue
For you and your nobles; nor need you dread
Slaughter of follower, stalwart or stripling,
Or death of earl, as of old you did.'
Into the hand of the aged leader,
The gray-haired hero, he gave the hilt,
The work of giants, the wonder of gold.
At the death of the demons the Danish lord
Took in his keeping the cunning craft,
The wondrous marvel, of mighty smiths;
When the world was freed of the ravaging fiend,
The foe of God, and his fearful dam
Marked with murder and badged with blood,
The bound hilt passed to the best of kings

[1655 -1685]

Who ever held sceptre beside two seas,
And dealt out treasure in Danish land!
    Hrothgar spoke, beholding the hilt,
The ancient relic whereon was etched
An olden record of struggle and strife,
The flood that ravaged the giant race,
The rushing deluge of ruin and death.
That evil kindred were alien to God,
But the Ruler avenged with the wrath of the deep!
On the hilt-guards, likewise, of gleaming gold
Was rightly carven in cunning runes,
Set forth and blazoned, for whom that blade,
With spiral tooling and twisted hilt,
That fairest of swords, was fashioned and smithied.
Then out spoke Hrothgar, Healfdene's son,
And all the retainers were silent and still:
'Well may he say, whose judgment is just,
Recalling to memory men of the past,
That this earl was born of a better stock!
Your fame, friend Beowulf, is blazoned abroad
Over all wide ways, and to every people.
In manful fashion have you showed your strength,
Your might and wisdom. My word I will keep,
The plighted friendship we formerly pledged.
Long shall you stand as a stay to your people,
A help to heroes, as Heremod was not
To the Honor-Scyldings, to Ecgwela's sons!
Not joy to kindred, but carnage and death,
He wrought as he ruled o'er the race of the Danes.
In savage anger he slew his comrades,
His table-companions, till, lawless and lone,

[1685-1715]

An odious outcast, he fled from men.
Though God had graced him with gifts of strength,
Over all men exalting him, still in his breast
A bloodthirsty spirit was rooted and strong.
He dealt not rings to the Danes for glory;
His lot was eternal torment of woe,
And lasting affliction. Learn from his fate!
Strive for virtue! I speak for your good;
In the wisdom of age I have told the tale.

    'Tis a wondrous marvel how mighty God
In gracious spirit bestows on men
The gift of wisdom, and goodly lands,
And princely power! He rules over all!
He suffers a man of lordly line
To set his heart on his own desires,
Awards him fullness of worldly joy,
A fair home-land, and the sway of cities,
The wide dominion of many a realm,
An ample kingdom, till, cursed with folly,
The thoughts of his heart take no heed of his end.
He lives in luxury, knowing not want,
Knowing no shadow of sickness or age;
No haunting sorrow darkens his spirit,
No hatred or discord deepens to war;
The world is sweet, to his every desire,
And evil assails not—until in his heart
Pride overpowering gathers and grows!
The warder slumbers, the guard of his spirit;
Too sound is that sleep, too sluggish the weight
Of worldly affairs, too pressing the Foe,
The Archer who looses the arrows of sin.

[1715-1744]

Then is his heart pierced, under his helm,
His soul in his bosom, with bitter dart.
He has no defense for the fierce assaults
Of the loathsome Fiend. What he long has cherished
Seems all too little! In anger and greed
He gives no guerdon of plated rings.
Since God has granted him glory and wealth
He forgets the future, unmindful of Fate.
But it comes to pass in the day appointed
His feeble body withers and fails;
Death descends, and another seizes﹣
His hoarded riches and rashly spends
The princely treasure, imprudent of heart.
Beloved Beowulf, best of warriors,
Avoid such evil and seek the good,
The heavenly wisdom. Beware of pride!
Now for a time you shall feel the fullness
And know the glory of strength, but soon
Sickness or sword shall strip you of might,
Or clutch of fire, or clasp of flood,
Or flight of arrow, or bite of blade,
Or relentless age; or the light of the eye
Shall darken and dim, and death on a sudden,
O lordly ruler, shall lay you low.

    A hundred half-years I've been head of the Ring-
  Danes,
Defending the folk against many a tribe
With spear-point and sword in the surges of battle
Till not one was hostile 'neath heaven's expanse.
But a loathsome change swept over the land,
Grief after gladness, when Grendel came,

[1745-1776]

That evil invader, that ancient foe!
Great sorrow of soul from his malice I suffered;
But thanks be to God who has spared me to see
His bloody head at the battle's end!
Join now in the banquet; have joy of the feast,
O mighty in battle! And the morrow shall bring
Exchange of treasure in ample store.'

Happy of heart the Geat leader hastened,
Took seat at the board as the good king bade.
Once more, as of old, brave heroes made merry
And tumult of revelry rose in the hall.

Then dark over men the night shadows deepened;
The host all arose, for Hrothgar was minded,
The gray, old Scylding, to go to his rest.
On Beowulf too, after labor of battle,
Came limitless longing and craving for sleep.
A hall-thane graciously guided the hero,
Weary and worn, to the place prepared,
Serving his wishes and every want
As befitted a mariner come from afar.
The stout-hearted warrior sank to his rest;
The lofty building, splendid and spacious,
Towered above him. His sleep was sound
Till the black-coated raven, blithesome of spirit,
Hailed the coming of Heaven's bliss.

✑[*The Parting of Beowulf and Hrothgar*]

Then over the shadows uprose the sun.
The Geats were in haste, and eager of heart
To depart to their people. Beowulf longed
To embark in his boat, to set sail for his home.

[1776-1806]

The hero tendered the good sword Hrunting
To the son of Ecglaf, bidding him bear
The lovely blade; gave thanks for the loan,
Called it a faithful friend in the fray,
Bitter in battle. The greathearted hero
Spoke no word in blame of the blade!
Arrayed in war-gear, and ready for sea,
The warriors bestirred them; and, dear to the Danes,
Beowulf sought the high seat of the king.
The gallant in war gave greeting to Hrothgar;
Beowulf spoke, the son of Ecgtheow:
'It is time at last to tell of our longing!
Our homes are far, and our hearts are fain
To seek again Hygelac over the sea.
You have welcomed us royally, harbored us well
As a man could wish; if I ever can win
Your affection more fully, O leader of heroes,
Swift shall you find me to serve you again!
If ever I learn, o'er the levels of ocean,
That neighboring nations beset you sore,
As in former days when foemen oppressed,
With thanes by the thousand I will hasten to help.
For I know that Hygelac, lord of the Geats,
Prince of the people, though young in years,
Will favor and further by word and deed
That my arm may aid you, and do you honor,
With stout ash-spear and succor of strength
In the press of need. And if princely Hrethric
Shall purpose to come to the court of the Geats,
He will find there a legion of loyal friends.
That man fares best to a foreign country

[1807–1839]

Who himself is stalwart and stout of heart.'
    Hrothgar addressed him, uttered his answer:
'Truly, these words has the Lord of wisdom
Set in your heart, for I never have harkened
To speech so sage from a man so young.
You have strength, and prudence, and wisdom of word!
I count it true if it come to pass
That point of spear in the press of battle,
Or deadly sickness, or stroke of sword,
Shall slay your leader, the son of Hrethel,
The prince of your people, and you still live,
The Sea-Geats could have no happier choice
If you would be willing to rule the realm,
As king to hold guard o'er the hoard and the heroes.
The longer I know you, the better I like you,
Beloved Beowulf! You have brought it to pass
That between our peoples a lasting peace
Shall bind the Geats to the Danish-born;
And strife shall vanish, and war shall cease,
And former feuds, while I rule this realm.
And many a man, in the sharing of treasure,
Shall greet another with goodly gifts
O'er the gannet's bath. And the ring-stemmed ship
Shall bear over ocean bountiful riches
In pledge of friendship. Our peoples, I know,
Shall be firm united toward foe and friend,
Faultless in all things, in fashion of old.'
    Then the son of Healfdene, shelter of earls,
Bestowed twelve gifts on the hero in hall,
Bade him in safety with bounty of treasure
Seek his dear people, and soon return.

[1839–1869]

The peerless leader, the Scylding lord,
Kissed the good thane and clasped to his bosom
While tears welled fast from the old man's eyes.
Both chances he weighed in his wise, old heart,
But greatly doubted if ever again
They should meet at council or drinking of mead.
Nor could Hrothgar master—so dear was the man—
His swelling sorrow; a yearning love
For the dauntless hero, deep in his heart,
Burned through his blood. Beowulf, the brave,
Prizing his treasure and proud of the gold,
Turned away, treading the grassy plain.
The ring-stemmed sea-goer, riding at anchor,
Awaited her lord. There was loud acclaim
Of Hrothgar's gifts, as they went their way.
He was a king without failing or fault,
Till old age, master of all mankind,
Stripped him of power and pride of strength.

◆§[Beowulf Returns to Geatland]

Then down to the sea came the band of the brave,
The host of young heroes in harness of war,
In their woven mail; and the coast-warden viewed
The heroes' return, as he heeded their coming!
No uncivil greeting he gave from the sea-cliff
As they strode to ship in their glistening steel;
But rode toward them and called their return
A welcome sight for their Weder kin.
There on the sand the ring-stemmed ship,
The broad-bosomed bark, was loaded with war-gear,
With horses and treasure; the mast towered high

[1870–1898]

Over the riches of Hrothgar's hoard.
A battle-sword Beowulf gave to the boatwarden
Hilted with gold; and thereafter in hall
He had the more honor because of the heirloom,
The shining treasure. The ship was launched.
Cleaving the combers of open sea
They dropped the shoreline of Denmark astern.
A stretching sea-cloth, a bellying sail,
Was bent on the mast; there was groaning of timbers;
A gale was blowing; the boat drove on.
The foamy-necked plunger plowed through the billows,
The ring-stemmed ship through the breaking seas,
Till at last they sighted the sea-cliffs of Geatland,
The well-known headlands; and, whipped by the wind,
The boat drove shoreward and beached on the sand.
    Straightway the harbor-watch strode to the seashore;
Long had he watched for the well-loved men,
Scanning the ocean with eager eyes!
The broad-bosomed boat he bound to the shingle
With anchor ropes, lest the rip of the tide
Should wrench from its mooring the comely craft.
    From the good ship Beowulf bade them bear
The precious jewels and plated gold,
The princely treasure. Not long was the path
That led to where Hygelac, son of Hrethel,
The giver of treasure, abode in his home
Hard by the sea-wall, hedged by his thanes.
Spacious the castle, splendid the king
On his high hall-seat; youthful was Hygd,
Wise and well-born—though winters but few
Hæreth's daughter had dwelt at court.

[1899-1929]

She was noble of spirit, not sparing in gifts
Of princely treasure to the people of the Geats.

*Of the pride of Thryth, and her crimes, the fair folk-queen
was free;*
Thryth, of whose liegemen none dared by day, save only her lord,
Lift up his eyes to her face, lest his fate be a mortal bondage,
Seizure and fetters and sword, a blow of the patterned blade
Declaring his doom, and proclaiming the coming of death.
That is no way of a queen, nor custom of lovely lady,
Though peerless her beauty and proud, that a weaver of peace
Should send a dear man to his death for a feigned affront.
But the kinsman of Hemming at last made an end of her evil.
For men at the drinking of mead tell tale of a change,
How she wrought less ruin and wrong when, given in marriage
Gleaming with jewels and gold, to the high-born hero and young,
Over the fallow flood she sailed, at her father's bidding
Seeking the land of Offa, and there while she lived,
Famed for goodness, fulfilled her fate on the throne.
She held high love for her lord, the leader of heroes,
The best, I have heard, of mankind or the children of men
Between the two seas; for Offa, the stalwart, was honored
For his gifts and his greatness in war. With wisdom he governed;
And from him Eomær descended, Hemming's kinsman, grandson
of Garmund,
Stalwart and strong in war, and the helper of heroes.

Then the hero strode with his stalwart band
Across the stretches of sandy beach,
The wide sea-shingle. The world-candle shone,
The hot sun hasting on high from the south.

[1929–1966]

Marching together they made their way
To where in his stronghold the stout young king,
Ongentheow's slayer, protector of earls,
Dispensed his treasure. Soon Hygelac heard
Of the landing of Beowulf, bulwark of men,
That his shoulder-companion had come to his court
Sound and safe from the strife of battle.

      The hall was prepared, as the prince gave bidding,
Places made ready for much travelled men.
And he who came safe from the surges of battle
Sat by the side of the king himself,
Kinsman by kinsman; in courtly speech
His liege lord greeted the loyal thane
With hearty welcome. And Hæreth's daughter
Passed through the hall-building pouring the mead,
With courtesy greeting the gathered host,
Bearing the cup to the hands of the heroes.
In friendly fashion in high-built hall
Hygelac questioned his comrade and thane;
For an eager longing burned in his breast
To hear from the Sea-Geats the tale of their travels.
'How did you fare in your far sea-roving,
Beloved Beowulf, in your swift resolve
To sail to the conflict, the combat in Heorot,
Across the salt waves? Did you soften at all
The sorrows of Hrothgar, the weight of his woe?
Deeply I brooded with burden of care
For I had no faith in this far sea-venture
For one so beloved. Long I implored
That you go not against the murderous monster,
But let the South Danes settle the feud

[1966–1997]

Themselves with Grendel. To God be thanks
That my eyes behold you unharmed and unhurt.'
    Beowulf spoke, the son of Ecgtheow:
'My dear lord Hygelac, many have heard
Of that famous grapple 'twixt Grendel and me,
The bitter struggle and strife in the hall
Where he formerly wrought such ruin and wrong,
Such lasting sorrow for Scylding men!
All that I avenged! Not any on earth
Who longest lives of that loathsome brood,
No kin of Grendel cloaked in his crime,
Has cause to boast of that battle by night!
First, in that country, I fared to the hall
With greeting for Hrothgar; Healfdene's kinsman
Learned all my purpose, assigned me a place
Beside his own son. 'Twas a happy host!
I never have seen under span of heaven
More mirth of heroes sitting at mead!
The peerless queen, the peace-pledge of peoples,
Passed on her round through the princely hall;
There was spurring of revels, dispensing of rings,
Ere the noble woman went to her seat.
    At times in the host the daughter of Hrothgar
Offered the beaker to earls in turn;
Freawaru men called her, the feasters in hall,
As she held out to heroes the well-wrought cup.
Youthful and gleaming with jewels of gold
To the fair son of Froda the maiden is plighted.
For the Scylding leader, the lord of the land,
Deems it wise counsel, accounting it gain,
To settle by marriage the murderous feud,

[1997–2028]

The bloody slaughter! But seldom for long
Does the spear go ungrasped when a prince has perished,
Though the bride in her beauty be peerless and proud!
Ill may it please the Heathobard prince
And all his thanes, when he leads his lady
Into the hall, that a Danish noble
Should be welcomed there by the Heathobard host.
For on him shall flash their forefathers' heirlooms,
Hard-edged, ring-hilted, the Heathobards' hoard
When of old they had war-might, nor wasted in battle
Their lives and the lives of their well-loved thanes.

Then an aged spearman shall speak at the beer-feast,
The treasure beholding with sorrow of heart,
Remembering sadly the slaughter of men,
Grimly goading the young hero's spirit,
Spurring to battle, speaking this word:
"Do you see, my lord, the sword of your father,
The blade he bore to the last of his fights,
The pride of his heart as, under his helmet,
The Scyldings slew him, the savage Danes,
When Withergyld fell, and after the slaughter,
The fall of heroes, they held the field?
And now a son of those bloody butchers,
Proud in his trappings, tramps into hall
And boasts of the killing, clothed with the treasure
That is yours by your birthright to have and to hold?"

Over and over the old man will urge him,
With cutting reminders recalling the past
Till it comes at last that the lady's thane,
For the deeds of his father, shall forfeit his life
In a bloody slaughter, slain by the sword,

[2029–2061]

While the slayer goes scatheless knowing the land.
On both sides then shall sword-oaths be broken
When hate boils up within Ingeld's heart,
And his love of his lady grows cooler and lessens
Because of his troubles. I count not true
Heathobard faith, nor their part in the peace,
Nor their friendship firm to the Danish folk.

I must now speak on, dispenser of treasure,
Further of Grendel, till fully you know
How we fared in that fierce and furious fight!
When the jewel of heaven had journeyed o'er earth,
The wrathful demon, the deadly foe,
Stole through the darkness spying us out
Where still unharmed we guarded the gold-hall.
But doom in battle and bitter death
Were Handscio's fate! He was first to perish
Though girded with weapon and famous in war.
Grendel murdered him, mangled his body,
Bolted the dear man's bloody corpse.
No sooner for that would the slaughterous spirit,
Bloody of tooth and brooding on evil,
Turn empty-handed away from the hall!
The mighty monster made trial of my strength
Clutching me close with his ready claw.
Wide and wondrous his huge pouch hung
Cunningly fastened, and fashioned with skill
From skin of dragon by devil's craft.
Therein the monster was minded to thrust me
Sinless and blameless, and many beside.
But it might not be, when I rose in wrath,
And fronted the hell-fiend face to face.

[2061-2092]

Too long is the tale how I took requital
On the cursed foe for his every crime,
But the deeds I did were a lasting honor,
Beloved prince, to your people's name.
He fled away, and a fleeting while
Possessed his life and the world's delights;
But he left in Heorot his severed hand,
A bloody reminder to mark his track.
Humbled in spirit and wretched in heart
Down he sank to the depths of the pool.
        When the morrow fell, and we feasted together,
The Scylding ruler rewarded me well
For the bloody strife, in guerdon bestowing
Goodly treasure of beaten gold.
There was song and revel. The aged Scylding
From well-stored mind spoke much of the past.
A warrior sang to the strains of the glee-wood,
Sometimes melodies mirthful and joyous,
Sometimes lays that were tragic and true.
And the great-hearted ruler at times would tell
A tale of wonder in fitting words.
Heavy with years the white-haired warrior
Grieved for his youth and the strength that was gone;
And his heart was moved by the weight of his winters
And many a memory out of the past.
All the long day we made merry together
Till another night came to the children of men,
And quickly the mother of Grendel was minded
To wreak her vengeance; raging with grief
She came to the hall where the hate of the Weders
Had slain her son. But the hideous hag

[2093–2120]

Avenged his killing; with furious clutch
She seized a warrior—the soul of Æschere,
Wise and aged, went forth from the flesh!
Not at all could the Danes, when the morrow dawned,
Set brand to his body or burn on the bale
Their well-loved comrade. With fiendish clasp
She carried his corpse through the fall of the force.
That was to Hrothgar, prince of the people,
Sorest of sorrows that ever befell!
For your sake the sad-hearted hero implored me
To prove my valor and, venturing life,
To win renown in the watery depths.
He promised reward. Full well is it known
How I humbled the horrible guard of the gulf.
Hand to hand for a space we struggled
Till the swirling eddies were stained with blood;
With cleaving sword-edge I severed the head
Of Grendel's hag in that hall of strife.
Not easily thence did I issue alive,
But my death was not fated; not yet was I doomed!
        Then the son of Healfdene, the shelter of earls,
Gave many a treasure to mark the deed.
The good king governed with courtly custom;
In no least way did I lose reward,
The meed of my might; but he gave me treasure,
Healfdene's son, to my heart's desire.
These riches I bring you, ruler of heroes,
And warmly tender with right good will.
Save for you, King Hygelac, few are my kinsmen,
Few are the favors but come from you.'
        Then he bade men bring the boar-crested headpiece,

[2121-2152]

The towering helmet, and steel-gray sark,
The splendid war-sword, and spoke this word:
'The good king Hrothgar gave me this gift,
This battle-armor, and first to you
Bade tell the tale of his friendly favor.
He said King Heorogar, lord of the Scyldings,
Long had worn it, but had no wish
To leave the mail to his manful son,
The dauntless Heoroweard, dear though he was!
Well may you wear it! Have joy of it all.'
As I've heard the tale, he followed the trappings
With four bay horses, matched and swift,
Graciously granting possession of both,
The steeds and the wealth. 'Tis the way of a kinsman,
Not weaving in secret the wiles of malice
Nor plotting the fall of a faithful friend.
To his kinsman Hygelac, hardy in war,
The heart of the nephew was trusty and true;
Dear to each was the other's good!
To Hygd, as I've heard, he presented three horses
Gaily saddled, slender and sleek,
And the gleaming necklace Wealhtheow gave,
A peerless gift from a prince's daughter.
With the gracious guerdon, the goodly jewel,
Her breast thereafter was well bedecked.
    So the son of Ecgtheow bore himself bravely,
Known for his courage and courteous deeds,
Strove after honor, slew not his comrades
In drunken brawling; nor brutal his mood.
But the bountiful gifts which the Lord God gave him
He held with a power supreme among men.

[2153-2183]

He had long been scorned, when the sons of the Geats
Accounted him worthless; the Weder lord
Held him not high among heroes in hall.
Laggard they deemed him, slothful and slack.
But time brought solace for all his ills!

  Then the battle-bold king, the bulwark of heroes,
Bade bring a battle-sword banded with gold,
The heirloom of Hrethel; no sharper steel,
No lovelier treasure, belonged to the Geats.
He laid the war-blade on Beowulf's lap,
Gave him a hall and a stately seat
And hides seven thousand. Inherited lands
Both held by birth-fee, home and estate.
But one held rule o'er the spacious realm,
And higher therein his order and rank.

[The Fire-Dragon and the Treasure]

  It later befell in the years that followed
After Hygelac sank in the surges of war,
And the sword slew Heardred under his shield
When the Battle-Scylfings, those bitter fighters,
Invaded the land of the victor-folk
Overwhelming Hereric's nephew in war,
That the kingdom came into Beowulf's hand.
For fifty winters he governed it well,
Aged and wise with the wisdom of years,
Till a fire-drake flying in darkness of night
Began to ravage and work his will.
On the upland heath he guarded a hoard,
A stone barrow lofty. Under it lay
A path concealed from the sight of men.

[2183–2214]

There a thief broke in on the heathen treasure,
Laid hand on a flagon all fretted with gold,
As the dragon discovered, though cozened in sleep
By the pilferer's cunning. The people soon found
That the mood of the dragon was roused to wrath!
        Not at all with intent, of his own free will,
Did he ravish the hoard, who committed the wrong;
But in dire distress the thrall of a thane,
A guilty fugitive fleeing the lash,
Forced his way in. There a horror befell him!
Yet the wretched exile escaped from the dragon,
Swift in retreat when the terror arose.
A flagon he took. There, many such treasures
Lay heaped in that earth-hall where the owner of old
Had carefully hidden the precious hoard,
The countless wealth of a princely clan.
Death came upon them in days gone by
And he who lived longest, the last of his line,
Guarding the treasure and grieving for friend,
Deemed it his lot that a little while only
He too might hold that ancient hoard.
A barrow new-built near the ocean billows
Stood cunningly fashioned beneath the cliff;
Into the barrow the ring-warden bore
The princely treasure, the precious trove
Of golden wealth, and these words he spoke:
'Keep thou, O Earth, what men could not keep—
This costly treasure—it came from thee!
Baleful slaughter has swept away,
Death in battle, the last of my blood;
They have lived their lives; they have left the mead-hall.

[2214-2252]

Now I have no one to wield the sword,
No one to polish the plated cup,
The precious flagon—the host is fled.
The hard-forged helmet fretted with gold
Shall be stripped of its inlay; the burnishers sleep
Whose charge was to brighten the battle-masks.
Likewise the corselet that countered in war
Mid clashing of bucklers the bite of the sword—
Corselet and warrior decay into dust;
Mailed coat and hero are moveless and still.
No mirth of gleewood, no music of harp,
No good hawk swinging in flight through the hall;
No swift steed stamps in the castle yard;
Death has ravished an ancient race.'
So sad of mood he bemoaned his sorrow,
Lonely and sole survivor of all,
Restless by day and wretched by night
Till the clutch of death caught at his heart.
Then the goodly treasure was found unguarded
By the venomous dragon enveloped in flame,
The old naked night-foe flying in darkness,
Haunting the barrows; a bane that brings
A fearful dread to the dwellers of earth.
His wont is to hunt out a hoard under ground
And guard heathen gold, growing old with the years.
But no whit for that is his fortune more fair!

    For three hundred winters this waster of peoples
Held the huge treasure-hall under the earth
Till the robber aroused him to anger and rage,
Stole the rich beaker and bore to his master,
Imploring his lord for a compact of peace.

[2252-2283]

So the hoard was robbed and its riches plundered;
To the wretch was granted the boon that he begged;
And his liege-lord first had view of the treasure,
The ancient work of the men of old.
Then the worm awakened and war was kindled,
The rush of the monster along the rock,
When the fierce one found the tracks of the foe;
He had stepped too close in his stealthy cunning
To the dragon's head. But a man undoomed
May endure with ease disaster and woe
If he has His favor who wields the world.
Swiftly the fire-drake sought through the plain
The man who wrought him this wrong in his sleep.
Inflamed and savage he circled the mound,
But the waste was deserted—no man was in sight.
The worm's mood was kindled to battle and war;
Time and again he returned to the barrow
Seeking the treasure-cup. Soon he was sure
That a man had plundered the precious gold.
Enraged and restless the hoard-warden waited
The gloom of evening. The guard of the mound
Was swollen with anger; the fierce one resolved
To requite with fire the theft of the cup.
Then the day was sped as the worm desired;
Lurking no longer within his wall
He sallied forth surrounded with fire,
Encircled with flame. For the folk of the land
The beginning was dread as the ending was grievous
That came so quickly upon their lord.
  ♦ Then the baleful stranger belched fire and flame,
Burned the bright dwellings—the glow of the blaze

[2283-2313]

Filled hearts with horror. The hostile flier
Was minded to leave there nothing alive.
From near and from far the war of the dragon,
The might of the monster, was widely revealed
So that all could see how the ravaging scather
Hated and humbled the Geatish folk.
Then he hastened back ere the break of dawn
To his secret den and the spoil of gold.
He had compassed the land with a flame of fire,
A blaze of burning; he trusted the wall,
The sheltering mound, and the strength of his might—
But his trust betrayed him! The terrible news
Was brought to Beowulf, told for a truth,
That his home was consumed in the surges of fire,
The goodly dwelling and throne of the Geats.
The heart of the hero was heavy with anguish,
The greatest of sorrows; in his wisdom he weened
He had grievously angered the Lord Everlasting,
Blamefully broken the ancient law.
Dark thoughts stirred in his surging bosom,
Welled in his breast, as was not his wont.
The flame of the dragon had levelled the fortress,
The people's stronghold washed by the wave.
But the king of warriors, prince of the Weders,
Exacted an ample revenge for it all.
The lord of warriors and leader of earls
Bade work him of iron a wondrous shield,
Knowing full well that wood could not serve him
Nor linden defend him against the flame.
The stalwart hero was doomed to suffer
The destined end of his days on earth;

[2314–2343]

Likewise the worm, though for many a winter
He had held his watch o'er the wealth of the hoard.
The ring-prince scorned to assault the dragon
With a mighty army, or host of men.
He feared not the combat, nor counted of worth
The might of the worm, his courage and craft,
Since often aforetime, beset in the fray,
He had safely issued from many an onset,
Many a combat and, crowned with success,
Purged of evil the hall of Hrothgar
And crushed out Grendel's loathsome kin.
      Nor was that the least of his grim engagements
When Hygelac fell, great Hrethel's son;
When the lord of the people, the prince of the Geats,
Died of his wounds in the welter of battle,
Perished in Friesland, smitten with swords.
Thence Beowulf came by his strength in swimming;
Thirty sets of armor he bore on his back
As he hasted to ocean. The Hetware men
Had no cause to boast of their prowess in battle
When they gathered against him with linden shields.
But few of them ever escaped his assault
Or came back alive to the homes they had left;
So the son of Ecgtheow swam the sea-stretches,
Lonely and sad, to the land of his kin.
Hygd then tendered him kingdom and treasure,
Wealth of riches and royal throne,
For she had no hope with Hygelac dead
That her son could defend the seat of his fathers
From foreign foemen. But even in need,
No whit the more could they move the hero

[2343-2374]

To be Heardred's liege, or lord of the land.
But he fostered Heardred with friendly counsel,
With honor and favor among the folk,
Till he came of age and governed the Geats.
Then the sons of Ohthere fleeing in exile
Sought out Heardred over the sea.
They had risen against the lord of the Scylfings,
Best of the sea-kings, bestower of rings,
An illustrious prince in the land of the Swedes.
So Heardred fell. For harboring exiles
The son of Hygelac died by the sword.
Ongentheow's son, after Heardred was slain,
Returned to his home, and Beowulf held
The princely power and governed the Geats.
He was a good king, grimly requiting
In later days the death of his prince.
Crossing the sea with a swarming host
He befriended Eadgils, Ohthere's son,
In his woe and affliction, with weapons and men;
He took revenge in a savage assault,
And slew the king. So Ecgtheow's son
Had come in safety through all his battles,
His bitter struggles and savage strife,
To the day when he fought with the deadly worm.
With eleven comrades, kindled to rage
The Geat lord went to gaze on the dragon.
Full well he knew how the feud arose,
The fearful affliction; for into his hold
From hand of finder the flagon had come.
✔ The thirteenth man in the hurrying throng
Was the sorrowful captive who caused the feud.

[2375-2408]

With woeful spirit and all unwilling
Needs must he guide them, for he only knew
Where the earth-hall stood near the breaking billows
Filled with jewels and beaten gold.
The monstrous warden, waiting for battle,
Watched and guarded the hoarded wealth.
No easy bargain for any of men
To seize that treasure! The stalwart king,
Gold-friend of Geats, took seat on the headland,
Hailed his comrades and wished them well.
Sad was his spirit, restless and ready,
And the march of Fate immeasurably near;
Fate that would strike, seek his soul's treasure,
And deal asunder the spirit and flesh.
Not long was his life encased in the body!
    ⌐ Beowulf spoke, the son of Ecgtheow:
'Many an ordeal I endured in youth,
And many a battle. I remember it all.
I was seven winters old when the prince of the people,
The lord of the treasure-hoard, Hrethel the king,
From the hand of my father had me and held me,
Recalling our kinship with treasure and feast.
As long as he lived I was no less beloved,
As thane in his hall, than the sons of his house,
Herebeald and Hæthcyn and Hygelac, my lord.
For the eldest brother the bed of death
Was foully fashioned by brother's deed
When Hæthcyn let fly a bolt from his horn-bow,
Missed the mark, and murdered his lord;
Brother slew brother with bloody shaft—
A tragic deed and beyond atonement,

[2408-2441]

A foul offense to sicken the heart!
Yet none the less was the lot of the prince
To lay down his soul and his life, unavenged.

    Even so sad and sorrowful is it,
And bitter to bear, to an old man's heart,
Seeing his young son swing on the gallows.
He wails his dirge and his wild lament
While his son hangs high, a spoil to the raven;
His aged heart can contrive no help.
Each dawn brings grief for the son that is gone
And his heart has no hope of another heir,
Seeing the one has gone to his grave.
In the house of his son he gazes in sorrow
On wine-hall deserted and swept by the wind,
Empty of joy. The horsemen and heroes
Sleep in the grave. No sound of the harp,
No welcoming revels as often of old!
He goes to his bed with his burden of grief;
To his spirit it seems that dwelling and land
Are empty and lonely, lacking his son.

    So the helm of the Weders yearned after Herebeald
And welling sadness surged in his heart.
He could not avenge the feud on the slayer
Nor punish the prince for the loathsome deed,
Though he loved him no longer, nor held him dear.
Because of this sorrow that sore befell
He left life's joys for the heavenly light,
Granting his sons, as a good man will,
Cities and land, when he went from the world.

    Then across the wide water was conflict and war,
A striving and struggle of Swedes and Geats,

[2442-2473]

A bitter hatred, when Hrethel died.
Ongentheow's sons were dauntless and daring,
Cared not for keeping of peace overseas;
But often around Hreosnabeorh slaughtered and slew.
My kinsmen avenged the feud and the evil,
As many have heard, though one of the Weders
Paid with his life—a bargain full bitter!
Hæthcyn's fate was to fall in the fight.
It is often recounted, a kinsman with sword-edge
Avenged in the morning the murderer's deed
When Ongentheow met Eofor. Helm split asunder;
The aged Scylfing sank down to his death.
The hand that felled him remembered the feud
And drew not back from the deadly blow.
      For all the rich gifts that Hygelac gave me
I repaid him in battle with shining sword,
As chance was given. He granted me land,
A gracious dwelling and goodly estate.
Nor needed he seek of the Gifths, or the Spear-Danes,
Or in Swedish land, a lesser in war
To fight for pay; in the press of battle
I was always before him alone in the van.
So shall I bear me while life-days last,
While the sword holds out that has served me well
Early and late since I slew Dæghrefn,
The Frankish hero, before the host.
He brought no spoil from the field of battle,
No corselet of mail to the Frisian king.
Not by the sword the warden of standards,
The stalwart warrior, fell in the fight.
My battle-grip shattered the bones of his body

[2474-2508]

And silenced the heart-beat. But now with the sword,
With hand and hard blade, I must fight for the treasure.'

❧[*Beowulf and Wiglaf Slay the Dragon*]

For the last time Beowulf uttered his boast:
'I came in safety through many a conflict
In the days of my youth; and now even yet,
Old as I am, I will fight this feud,
Do manful deeds, if the dire destroyer
Will come from his cavern to meet my sword.'
The king for the last time greeted his comrades,
Bold helmet-bearers and faithful friends:
'I would bear no sword nor weapon to battle
With the evil worm, if I knew how else
I could close with the fiend, as I grappled with Grendel.
From the worm I look for a welling of fire,
A belching of venom, and therefore I bear
Shield and byrny. Not one foot's space
Will I flee from the monster, the ward of the mound.
It shall fare with us both in the fight at the wall
As Fate shall allot, the lord of mankind.
Though bold in spirit, I make no boast
As I go to fight with the flying serpent.
Clad in your corselets and trappings of war,
By the side of the barrow abide you to see
Which of us twain may best after battle
Survive his wounds. Not yours the adventure,
Nor the mission of any, save mine alone,
To measure his strength with the monstrous dragon
And play the part of a valiant earl.
By deeds of daring I'll gain the gold

[2508–2536]

Or death in battle shall break your lord.'
    Then the stalwart rose with his shield upon him,
Bold under helmet, bearing his sark
Under the stone-cliff; he trusted the strength
Of his single might. Not so does a coward!
He who survived through many a struggle,
Many a combat and crashing of troops,
Saw where a stone-arch stood by the wall
And a gushing stream broke out from the barrow.
Hot with fire was the flow of its surge,
Nor could any abide near the hoard unburned,
Nor endure its depths, for the flame of the dragon.
Then the lord of the Geats in the grip of his fury
Gave shout of defiance; the strong-heart stormed.
His voice rang out with the rage of battle,
Resounding under the hoary stone.
— Hate was aroused; the hoard-warden knew
'Twas the voice of a man. No more was there time
To sue for peace; the breath of the serpent,
A blast of venom, burst from the rock.
The ground resounded; the lord of the Geats
Under the barrow swung up his shield
To face the dragon; the coiling foe
Was gathered to strike in the deadly strife.
The stalwart hero had drawn his sword,
His ancient heirloom of tempered edge;
In the heart of each was fear of the other!
The shelter of kinsmen stood stout of heart
Under towering shield as the great worm coiled;
Clad in his war-gear he waited the rush.
In twisting folds the flame-breathing dragon

[2536–2569]

Sped to its fate. The shield of the prince
For a lesser while guarded his life and his body
Than heart had hoped. For the first time then
It was not his portion to prosper in war;
Fate did not grant him glory in battle!
Then lifted his arm the lord of the Geats
And smote the worm with his ancient sword
But the brown edge failed as it fell on bone,
And cut less deep than the king had need
In his sore distress. Savage in mood
The ward of the barrow countered the blow
With a blast of fire; wide sprang the flame.
The ruler of Geats had no reason to boast;
His unsheathed iron, his excellent sword,
Had weakened as it should not, had failed in the fight.
It was no easy journey for Ecgtheow's son
To leave this world and against his will
Find elsewhere a dwelling! So every man shall
In the end give over this fleeting life.

    Not long was the lull. Swiftly the battlers
Renewed their grapple. The guard of the hoard
Grew fiercer in fury. His venomous breath
Beat in his breast. Enveloped in flame
The folk-leader suffered a sore distress.
No succoring band of shoulder-companions,
No sons of warriors aided him then
By valor in battle. They fled to the forest
To save their lives; but a sorrowful spirit
Welled in the breast of one of the band.
The call of kinship can never be stilled
In the heart of a man who is trusty and true.

[2570–2601]

His name was Wiglaf, Weohstan's son,
A prince of the Scylfings, a peerless thane,
Ælfhere's kinsman; he saw his king
Under his helmet smitten with heat.
He thought of the gifts which his lord had given,
The wealth and the land of the Wægmunding line
And all the folk-rights his father had owned;
Nor could he hold back, but snatched up his buckler,
His linden shield and his ancient sword,
Heirloom of Eanmund, Ohthere's son,
Whom Weohstan slew with the sword in battle,
Wretched and friendless and far from home.
The brown-hewed helmet he bore to his kinsmen,
The ancient blade and the byrny of rings.
These Onela gave him—his nephew's arms—
Nor called for vengeance, nor fought the feud,
Though Weohstan had slaughtered his brother's son.
He held the treasures for many half-years,
The byrny and sword, till his son was of age
For manful deeds, as his father before him.
Among the Geats he gave him of war-gear
Countless numbers of every kind;
Then, full of winters, he left the world,
Gave over this life. And Wiglaf, the lad,
Was to face with his lord the first of his battles,
The hazard of war. But his heart did not fail
Nor the blade of his kinsman weaken in war,
As the worm soon found when they met in the fight!
      Wiglaf spoke in sorrow of soul,
With bitter reproach rebuking his comrades:
'I remember the time, as we drank in the mead-hall,

[2602-2633]

When we swore to our lord who bestowed these rings
That we would repay for the war-gear and armor,
The hard swords and helmets, if need like this
Should ever befall him. He chose us out
From all the host for this high adventure,
Deemed us worthy of glorious deeds,
Gave me these treasures, regarded us all
As high-hearted bearers of helmet and spear—
Though our lord himself, the shield of his people,
Thought single-handed to finish this feat,
Since of mortal men his measure was most
Of feats of daring and deeds of fame.
Now is the day that our lord has need
Of the strength and courage of stalwart men.
Let us haste to succor his sore distress
In the horrible heat and the merciless flame.
God knows I had rather the fire should enfold
My body and limbs with my gold-friend and lord.
Shameful it seems that we carry our shields
Back to our homes ere we harry the foe
And ward the life of the Weder king.
Full well I know it is not his due
That he alone, of the host of the Geats,
Should suffer affliction and fall in the fight.
One helmet and sword, one byrny and shield,
Shall serve for us both in the storm of strife.'
Then Wiglaf dashed through the deadly reek
In his battle-helmet to help his lord.
Brief were his words: 'Beloved Beowulf,
Summon your strength, remember the vow
You made of old in the years of youth

[2634-2664]

Not to allow your glory to lessen
As long as you lived. With resolute heart,
And dauntless daring, defend your life
With all your force. I fight at your side!'

⸜Once again the worm, when the words were spoken,
The hideous foe in a horror of flame,
Rushed in rage at the hated men.
Wiglaf's buckler was burned to the boss
In the billows of fire; his byrny of mail
Gave the young hero no help or defense.
But he stoutly pressed on under shield of his kinsman
When his own was consumed in the scorching flame.
Then the king once more was mindful of glory,
Swung his great sword-blade with all his might
And drove it home on the dragon's head.
But Nægling broke, it failed in the battle,
The blade of Beowulf, ancient and gray.
It was not his lot that edges of iron
Could help him in battle; his hand was too strong,
Overtaxed, I am told, every blade with its blow.
Though he bore a wondrous hard weapon to war,
No whit the better was he thereby!

⸜A third time then the terrible scather,
The monstrous dragon inflamed with the feud,
Rushed on the king when the opening offered,
Fierce and flaming; fastened its fangs
In Beowulf's throat; he was bloodied with gore;
His life-blood streamed from the welling wound.

As they tell the tale, in the king's sore need
His shoulder-companion showed forth his valor,
His craft and courage, and native strength.

[2665-2696]

To the head of the dragon he paid no heed,
Though his hand was burned as he helped his king.
A little lower the stalwart struck
At the evil beast, and his blade drove home
Plated and gleaming. The fire began
To lessen and wane. The king of the Weders
Summoned his wits; he drew the dagger
He wore on his corselet, cutting and keen,
And slit asunder the worm with the blow.
So they felled the foe and wrought their revenge;
The kinsmen together had killed the dragon.
So a man should be when the need is bitter!
That was the last fight Beowulf fought;
That was the end of his work in the world.

✑§[*Beowulf's Death*]

✑ The wound which the dragon had dealt him began
To swell and burn; and soon he could feel
The baneful venom inflaming his breast.
The wise, old warrior sank down by the wall
And stared at the work of the giants of old,
The arches of stone and the standing columns
Upholding the ancient earth-hall within.
His loyal thane, the kindest of comrades,
Saw Beowulf bloody and broken in war;
In his hands bore water and bathed his leader,
And loosened the helm from his dear lord's head.

Beowulf spoke, though his hurt was sore,
The wounds of battle grievous and grim.
Full well he weened that his life was ended,
And all the joy of his years on earth;

[2697-2727]

That his days were done, and Death most near:
'My armor and sword I would leave to my son
Had Fate but granted, born of my body,
An heir to follow me after I'm gone.
For fifty winters I've ruled this realm,
And never a lord of a neighboring land
Dared strike with terror or seek with sword.
In my life I abode by the lot assigned,
Kept well what was mine, courted no quarrels,
Swore no false oaths. And now for all this
Though my hurt is grievous, my heart is glad.
When life leaves body, the Lord of mankind
Cannot lay to my charge the killing of kinsmen!
Go quickly, dear Wiglaf, to gaze on the gold
Beneath the hoar stone. The dragon lies still
In the slumber of death, despoiled of his hoard.
Make haste that my eyes may behold the treasure,
The gleaming jewels, the goodly store,
And, glad of the gold, more peacefully leave
The life and the realm I have ruled so long.'
      Then Weohstan's son, as they tell the tale,
Clad in his corselet and trappings of war,
Hearkened at once to his wounded lord.
Under roof of the barrow he broke his way.
Proud in triumph he stood by the seat,
Saw glittering jewels and gold on the ground,
The den of the dragon, the old dawn-flier,
And all the wonders along the walls.
Great bowls and flagons of bygone men
Lay all unburnished and barren of gems,
Many a helmet ancient and rusted,

[2727-2763]

Many an arm-ring cunningly wrought.
Treasure and gold, though hid in the ground,
Override man's wishes, hide them who will!
High o'er the hoard he beheld a banner,
Greatest of wonders, woven with skill,
All wrought of gold; its radiance lighted
The vasty ground and the glittering gems.
But no sign of the worm! The sword-edge had slain him.
As I've heard the tale, the hero unaided
Rifled those riches of giants of old,
The hoard in the barrow, and heaped in his arms
Beakers and platters, picked what he would
And took the banner, the brightest of signs.
The ancient sword with its edge of iron
Had slain the worm who watched o'er the wealth,
In the midnight flaming, with menace of fire
Protecting the treasure for many a year
Till he died the death. Then Wiglaf departed
In haste returning enriched with spoil.
He feared, and wondered if still he would find
The lord of the Weders alive on the plain,
Broken and weary and smitten with wounds.
With his freight of treasure he found the prince,
His dear lord, bloody and nigh unto death.
With water he bathed him till words broke forth
From the hoard of his heart and, aged and sad,
Beowulf spoke, as he gazed on the gold:
'For this goodly treasure whereon I gaze
I give my thanks to the Lord of all,
To the Prince of glory, Eternal God,
Who granted me grace to gain for my people

[2763–2797]

Such dower of riches before my death.
I gave my life for this golden hoard.
Heed well the wants, the need of my people;
My hour is come, and my end is near.
Bid warriors build, when they burn my body,
A stately barrow on the headland's height.
It shall be for remembrance among my people
As it towers high on the Cape of the Whale,
And sailors shall know it as Beowulf's Barrow,
Sea-faring mariners driving their ships
Through fogs of ocean from far countries.'
Then the great-hearted king unclasped from his throat
A collar of gold, and gave to his thane;
Gave the young hero his gold-decked helmet,
His ring and his byrny, and wished him well.
'You are the last of the Wægmunding line.
All my kinsmen, earls in their glory,
Fate has sent to their final doom,
And I must follow.' These words were the last
The old king spoke ere the pyre received him,
The leaping flames of the funeral blaze,
And his breath went forth from his bosom, his soul
Went forth from the flesh, to the joys of the just.
     Then bitter it was for Beowulf's thane
To behold his loved one lying on earth
Suffering sore at the end of life.
The monster that slew him, the dreadful dragon,
Likewise lay broken and brought to his death.
The worm no longer could rule the hoard,
But the hard, sharp sword, the work of the hammer,
Had laid him low; and the winged dragon

[2798–2830]

Lay stretched near the barrow, broken and still.
No more in the midnight he soared in air,
Disclosing his presence, and proud of his gold;
For he sank to earth by the sword of the king.
But few of mankind, if the tales be true,
Has it prospered much, though mighty in war
And daring in deed, to encounter the breath
Of the venomous worm or plunder his wealth
When the ward of the barrow held watch o'er the mound.
Beowulf bartered his life for the treasure;
Both foes had finished this fleeting life.

    Not long was it then till the laggards in battle
Came forth from the forest, ten craven in fight,
Who had dared not face the attack of the foe
In their lord's great need. The shirkers in shame
Came wearing their bucklers and trappings of war
Where the old man lay. They looked upon Wiglaf.
Weary he sat by the side of his leader
Attempting with water to waken his lord.
It availed him little; the wish was vain!
He could not stay his soul upon earth,
Nor one whit alter the will of God.
The Lord ruled over the lives of men
As He rules them still. With a stern rebuke
He reproached the cowards whose courage had failed.
Wiglaf addressed them, Weohstan's son;
Gazed sad of heart on the hateful men:
'Lo! he may say who would speak the truth
That the lord who gave you these goodly rings,
This warlike armor wherein you stand—
When oft on the ale-bench he dealt to his hall-men

[2830–2868]

Helmet and byrny, endowing his thanes
With the fairest he found from near or from far—
That he grievously wasted these trappings of war
When battle befell him. The king of the folk
Had no need to boast of his friends in the fight.
But the God of victory granted him strength
To avenge himself with the edge of the sword
When he needed valor. Of little avail
The help I brought in the bitter battle!
Yet still I strove, though beyond my strength,
To aid my kinsman. And ever the weaker
The savage foe when I struck with my sword;
Ever the weaker the welling flame!
Too few defenders surrounded our ruler
When the hour of evil and terror befell.
Now granting of treasure and giving of swords,
Inherited land-right and joy of the home,
Shall cease from your kindred. And each of your clan
Shall fail of his birthright when men from afar
Hear tell of your flight and your dastardly deed.
Death is better for every earl
Than life besmirched with the brand of shame!'

[The Messenger Foretells the Doom of the Geats]

Than Wiglaf bade tell the tidings of battle
Up over the cliff in the camp of the host
Where the linden-bearers all morning long
Sat wretched in spirit, and ready for both,
The return, or the death, of their dear-loved lord.
Not long did he hide, who rode up the headland,
The news of their sorrow, but spoke before all:

[2868-2899]

'Our leader lies low, the lord of the Weders,
The king of the Geats, on the couch of death.
He sleeps his last sleep by the deeds of the worm.
The dreadful dragon is stretched beside him
Slain with dagger-wounds. Not by the sword
Could he quell the monster or lay him low.
And Wiglaf is sitting, Weohstan's son,
Bent over Beowulf, living by dead.
Death watch he keeps in sorrow of spirit
Over the bodies of friend and foe.

Now comes peril of war when this news is rumored abroad,
The fall of our king known afar among Frisians and Franks!
For a fierce feud rose with the Franks when Hygelac's warlike host
Invaded the Frisian fields, and the Hetware vanquished the Geats,
Overcame with the weight of their hordes, and Hygelac fell in the
  fray;
It was not his lot to live on dispensing the spoils of war.
And never since then of the Franks had we favor or friend.

  And I harbor no hope of peace or faith from the Swedish folk,
For well is it known of men that Ongentheow slew with the sword
Hæthcyn, the son of Hrethel, near Ravenswood, in the fight
When the Swedish people in pride swept down on the Geats.
And Ohthere's aged father, old and a terror in battle,
Made onslaught, killing their king, and rescued his queen,
Ohthere's mother and Onela's, aged, bereft of her gold.
He followed the flying foe till, lordless and lorn,
They barely escaped into Ravenswood. There he beset them,
A wretched remnant of war, and weary with wounds.
And all the long hours of the night he thundered his threats
That some on the morrow he would slay with the edge of the sword,

[2900–2940]

And some should swing on the gallows for food for the fowls!
But hope returned with the dawn to the heavy-hearted
When they heard the sound of the trumpets and Hygelac's horn,
As the good king came with his troops marching up on their track.
  Then was a gory meeting of Swedes and Geats;
On all sides carnage and slaughter, savage and grim,
As the struggling foemen grappled and swayed in the fight.
And the old earl Ongentheow, crestfallen and cowed,
Fled with his men to a fastness, withdrew to the hills.
He had tasted Hygelac's strength, the skill of the hero in war,
And he had no hope to resist or strive with the sea-men,
To save his hoard from their hands, or his children, or wife.
So the old king fled to his fortress; but over the plain
Hygelac's banners swept on in pursuit of the Swedes,
Stormed to the stronghold's defenses, and old Ongentheow
Was brought to bay with the sword, and subject to Eofor's will!
Wulf, son of Wonred, in wrath then struck with his sword,
And the blood in streams burst forth from under the old man's hair.
Yet the aged Scylfing was all undaunted and answered the stroke
With a bitter exchange in the battle; and Wonred's brave son
Could not requite the blow, for the hero had cleft his helmet,
And, covered with blood, he was forced to bow; he fell to the earth.
But his death was not doomed, and he rallied, though the wound
 was deep.
Then Hygelac's hardy thane, when his brother lay low,
Struck with his ancient blade, a sturdy sword of the giants,
Cut through the shield-wall, cleaving the helmet. The king,
The folk-defender, sank down. He was hurt unto death.
Then were many that bound Wulf's wounds when the fight was
 won,
When the Geats held the ground of battle; as booty of war

[2940–2984]

Eofor stripped Ongentheow of iron byrny and helm,
Of sword-blade hilted and hard, and bore unto Hygelac
The old man's trappings of war. And Hygelac took the treasures,
Promising fair rewards, and this he fulfilled.
The son of Hrethel, the king of the Geats, when he came to his
* home,*
Repaid with princely treasure the prowess of Eofor and Wulf;
Gave each an hundred thousand of land and linked rings,
And none could belittle or blame. They had won the honor in war.
He gave to Eofor also the hand of his only daughter
To be a pledge of good will, and the pride of his home.

This is the fighting and this the feud,
The bitter hatred, that breeds the dread
Lest the Swedish people should swarm against us
Learning our lord lies lifeless and still.
His was the hand that defended the hoard,
Heroes, and realm against ravaging foe,
By noble counsel and dauntless deed.
Let us go quickly to look on the king
Who brought us treasure, and bear his corpse
To the funeral pyre. The precious hoard
Shall burn with the hero. There lies the heap
Of untold treasure so grimly gained,
Jewels and gems he bought with his blood
At the end of life. All these at the last
The flames shall veil and the brands devour.
No man for remembrance shall take from the treasure,
Nor beauteous maiden adorn her breast
With gleaming jewel; bereft of gold
And tragic-hearted many shall tread

[2985-3019]

A foreign soil, now their lord has ceased
From laughter and revel and rapture of joy.
Many a spear in the cold of morning
Shall be borne in hand uplifted on high.
No sound of harp shall waken the warrior,
But the dusky raven despoiling the dead
Shall clamor and cry and call to the eagle
What fare he found at the carrion-feast
The while with the wolf he worried the corpses.'
    So the stalwart hero had told his tidings,
His fateful message; nor spoke amiss
As to truth or telling. The host arose;
On their woeful way to the Eagles' Ness
They went with tears to behold the wonder.
They found the friend, who had dealt them treasure
In former days, on the bed of death,
Stretched out lifeless upon the sand.
The last of the good king's days was gone;
Wondrous the death of the Weder prince!
They had sighted first, where it lay outstretched,
The monstrous wonder, the loathsome worm,
The horrible fire-drake, hideous-hued,
Scorched with the flame. The spread of its length
Was fifty foot-measures! Oft in the night
It sported in air, then sinking to earth
Returned to its den. Now moveless in death
It had seen the last of its earthly lair.
Beside the dragon were bowls and beakers,
Platters lying, and precious swords
Eaten with rust, where the hoard had rested

[3019-3049]

A thousand winters in the womb of earth.
That boundless treasure of bygone men,
The golden dower, was girt with a spell
So that never a man might ravage the ring-hall
Save as God himself, the Giver of victory—
He is the Shelter and Shield of men—
Might allow such man as seemed to Him meet,
Might grant whom He would, to gather the treasure.

    His way of life, who had wickedly hoarded
The wealth of treasure beneath the wall,
Had an evil end, as was widely seen.
Many the dragon had sent to death,
But in fearful fashion the feud was avenged!
'Tis a wondrous thing when a warlike earl
Comes to the close of his destined days,
When he may no longer among his kinsmen
Feast in the mead-hall. So Beowulf fared
When he sought the dragon in deadly battle!
Himself he knew not what fate was in store
Nor the coming end of his earthly life.
The lordly princes who placed the treasure
Had cursed it deep to the day of doom,
That the man who plundered and gathered the gold
Might pay for the evil imprisoned in hell,
Shackled in torment and punished with pain,
Except the invader should first be favored
With the loving grace of the Lord of all!

    Then spoke Wiglaf, Weohstan's son:
'Often for one man many must sorrow
As has now befallen the folk of the Geats.

[3049–3078]

We could not persuade the king by our counsel,
Our well-loved leader, to shun assault
On the dreadful dragon guarding the gold;
To let him lie where he long had lurked
In his secret lair till the world shall end.
But Beowulf, dauntless, pressed to his doom.
The hoard was uncovered; heavy the cost;
Too strong the fate that constrained the king!
I entered the barrow, beholding the hoard
And all the treasure throughout the hall;
In fearful fashion the way was opened,
An entrance under the wall of earth.
Of the hoarded treasure I heaped in my arms
A weighty burden, and bore to my king.
He yet was living; his wits were clear.
Much the old man said in his sorrow;
Sent you greeting, and bade you build
In the place of burning a lofty barrow,
Proud and peerless, to mark his deeds;
For he was of all men the worthiest warrior
In all the earth, while he still might rule
And wield the wealth of his lordly land.
Let us haste once more to behold the treasure,
The gleaming wonders beneath the wall.
I will show the way that you all may see
And closely scan the rings and the gold.
Let the bier be ready, the pyre prepared,
When we come again to carry our lord,
Our leader beloved, where long he shall lie
In the kindly care of the Lord of all.'

[3079–3109]

↬[*Beowulf's Funeral*]

Then the son of Weohstan, stalwart in war,
Bade send command to the heads of homes
To bring from afar the wood for the burning
Where the good king lay: 'Now glede shall devour,
As dark flame waxes, the warrior prince
Who has often withstood the shower of steel
When the storm of arrows, sped from the string,
Broke over shield, and shaft did service,
With feather-fittings guiding the barb.'
   Then the wise son of Weohstan chose from the host
Seven thanes of the king, the best of the band;
Eight heroes together they hied to the barrow
In under the roof of the fearful foe;
One of the warriors leading the way
Bore in his hand a burning brand.
They cast no lots who should loot the treasure
When they saw unguarded the gold in the hall
Lying there useless; little they scrupled
As quickly they plundered the precious store.
Over the sea-cliff into the ocean
They tumbled the dragon, the deadly worm,
Let the sea-tide swallow the guarder of gold.
Then a wagon was loaded with well-wrought treasure,
A countless number of every kind;
And the aged warrior, the white-haired king,
Was borne on high to the Cape of the Whale.
   The Geat folk fashioned a peerless pyre
Hung round with helmets and battle-boards,
With gleaming byrnies as Beowulf bade.

[3110–3140]

In sorrow of soul they laid on the pyre
Their mighty leader, their well-loved lord.
The warriors kindled the bale on the barrow,
Wakened the greatest of funeral fires.
Dark o'er the blaze the wood-smoke mounted;
The winds were still, and the sound of weeping
Rose with the roar of the surging flame
Till the heat of the fire had broken the body.
With hearts that were heavy they chanted their sorrow,
Singing a dirge for the death of their lord;
And an aged woman with upbound locks
Lamented for Beowulf, wailing in woe.
Over and over she uttered her dread
Of sorrow to come, of bloodshed and slaughter,
Terror of battle, and bondage, and shame.
The smoke of the bale-fire rose to the sky!
    The men of the Weder folk fashioned a mound
Broad and high on the brow of the cliff,
Seen from afar by seafaring men.
Ten days they worked on the warrior's barrow
Inclosing the ash of the funeral flame
With a wall as worthy as wisdom could shape.
They bore to the barrow the rings and the gems,
The wealth of the hoard the heroes had plundered.
The olden treasure they gave to the earth,
The gold to the ground, where it still remains
As useless to men as it was of yore.
Then round the mound rode the brave in battle,
The sons of warriors, twelve in a band,
Bemoaning their sorrow and mourning their king.
They sang their dirge and spoke of the hero

[3141-3172]

Vaunting his valor and venturous deeds.
So is it proper a man should praise
His friendly lord with a loving heart,
When his soul must forth from the fleeting flesh.
So the folk of the Geats, the friends of his hearth,
Bemoaned the fall of their mighty lord;
Said he was kindest of worldly kings,
Mildest, most gentle, most eager for fame.

[3173-3182]

A SELECTED BIBLIOGRAPHY

A SELECTED BIBLIOGRAPHY

THE reader who wishes to follow the development of scholarly opinion on important problems in the *Beowulf,* or who desires information on the detailed and special questions with which the poem abounds, may consult the full and classified bibliographies in the volumes of Chambers (to 1930) and Klaeber (to 1936), both noted below. For articles and books published since 1936, the student may consult the appropriate sections of the following annual publications: *The Year's Work in English Studies* (Oxford University Press); the *Annual Bibliography of English Language and Literature* (Cambridge University Press).

To facilitate use of the books and articles listed below, they are presented in chronological order in their respective groups.

I. THE OLD ENGLISH TEXT

FACSIMILE

Zupitza, J., *Autotypes of the unique Cotton MS. Vitellius A xv,* with a transliteration and notes. Early English Text Society, no. 77 (London, 1882).

CONCORDANCE

Cook, A. S., *A Concordance to Beowulf* (Halle, 1911).

EDITIONS

Holthausen, F., *Beowulf nebst dem Finnsburg-Bruchstück.* i. Texte; ii. Einleitung, Glossar und Anmerkungen (Heidelberg, 1905–6). 6th edition of the text, to which have been added *Waldere, Deor, Widsith,* and the German *Hildebrandslied*; 5th edition of the introduction, glossary and notes (Heidelberg, 1929).

Schücking, L. L., *Beowulf,* based on Heyne's text (Paderborn, 1908; editions and reprints to 14th edition, 1931).

Sedgefield, W. J., *Beowulf,* edited with introduction, bibliography, notes, glossary, and appendices (Manchester, 1910; 3rd edition, revised, 1935).

Wyatt, A. J., and Chambers, R. W., *Beowulf, with the Finnsburg Fragment,* revision of Wyatt's edition of 1894 and 1898 (Cambridge, Eng., 1914; 2nd edition, 1920).

Klaeber, Fr., *Beowulf and the Fight at Finnsburg,* with introduction, bibliography, notes, glossary, and appendices (Boston, 1922; 3rd edition, enlarged and re-set, 1936).

II. Translations

For a review of translations, and for discussions of the suitability of prose and of various verse-forms in translating the *Beowulf,* see Klaeber's bibliography (1936), pp.cxxxiv–cxxxv.

IN VERSE

Morris, W., and Wyatt, A. J., *The Tale of Beowulf.* Kelmscott Press (Hammersmith, 1895; 2nd edition, London, 1898). Imitative metre, archaic diction.

Gummere, F. B., *The Oldest English Epic* (New York, 1909). In alliterative verse. Contains also *Finnsburg, Waldere, Deor, Widsith,* and the German *Hildebrand.* Also in the Harvard Classics, vol.49 (1910).

Hall, J. R. Clark, *Beowulf* (Cambridge, Eng., 1914). In four-stress lines, without alliteration.

Spaeth, J. D., *Old English Poetry* (Princeton, 1922). In alliterative verse, with prose summaries of the episodes.

Leonard, W. E., *Beowulf* (New York, 1923). In meter imitating the Nibelungen couplet.

Strong, A., *Beowulf* (London, 1925). In the long rhymed couplets used by Morris in *Sigurd the Volsung.*

Gerould, G. H., *Beowulf and Sir Gawain and the Green Knight* (New York, 1933). In alliterative verse.

IN PROSE

Hall, J. R. Clark, *Beowulf and the Fight at Finnsburg* (London, 1901; revised edition, 1911).

Tinker, C. B., *Beowulf* (Boston, 1902; revised edition, 1910).

Child, C. G., *Beowulf and the Finnesburg Fragment,* in Riverside Literature Series, no.159 (Boston, 1904).

Gordon, R. K., *The Song of Beowulf* (New York, 1923). Also in Gordon's *Anglo-Saxon Poetry,* Everyman's Library (New York, 1926).

III. CRITICAL STUDIES

GENERAL TREATMENTS

Bradley, H., 'Beowulf,' in *Encyclopaedia Britannica,* vol.3, 11th to 14th editions.

Wülker, R., *Grundriss zur Geschichte der angelsächsischen Litteratur,* pp.244–315 (Leipzig, 1885).

Brooke, S. A., *History of Early English Literature,* i,17–131 (London, 1892). See also his *English Literature from the Beginning to the Norman Conquest,* pp.58–83 (London, 1898).

Chadwick, H. M., 'Early National Poetry,' in *Cambridge History of English Literature,* i,22–32 (Cambridge, Eng., 1907).

Brandl, A., 'Englische Literatur: Angelsächsische Periode,' in Paul's *Grundriss,* 2nd edition, ii,988–1024. Also separately as *Geschichte der altenglischen Literatur* (Strassburg, 1908).

Chambers, R. W., *Beowulf, an introduction to the study of the poem, with a discussion of the stories of Offa and Finn* (Cambridge, Eng., 1921; revised edition, 1932). The standard treatise on *Beowulf.*

Klaeber, Fr. (see above, under Editions). The introduction (pp.ix–cxxiv) presents, under eight heads, a comprehensive and compact account of the poem.

Lawrence, W. W., *Beowulf and Epic Tradition* (Cambridge, Mass., 1928). Especially valuable for the picture of Germanic life behind the poem

Hoops, J., *Beowulfstudien* (Heidelberg, 1932) and *Kommentar zum Beowulf* (Heidelberg, 1932). Companion volumes comprising an extremely useful commentary on the text of the poem.

STUDIES IN BACKGROUND

Gummere, F. B., *Germanic Origins* (New York, 1892). Reissued as *Founders of England,* with supplementary notes by F.P. Magoun (New York, 1930).

Ker, W. P., *Epic and Romance* (London, 1897).

Jiriczek, O. L., *Northern Hero Legends* (London, 1902). Translation by M.Bentinck Smith of 2nd edition of Jiriczek's *Die Deutsche Heldensage* (Leipzig, 1897).

Hart, W. M., *Ballad and Epic.* Harvard Studies and Notes in Philology and Literature, vol.11 (Boston, 1907).

Dale, E., *National Life and Character in the Mirror of Early English Literature* (Cambridge, Eng., 1907).

Panzer, F., *Studien zur germanischen Sagengeschichte. I. Beowulf* (Munich, 1910).

Hoops, J. (editor), *Reallexikon der germanischen Altertumskunde,* 4 vols. (Strassburg, 1911–19).

Chadwick, H. M., *The Heroic Age* (Cambridge, Eng., 1912).

Chambers, R. W., *Widsith, a Study in Old English Heroic Legend* (Cambridge, Eng., 1912).

Dickins, Bruce, *Runic and Heroic Poems of the Old Teutonic Peoples* (Cambridge, Eng., 1915).

Olrik, A., *The Heroic Legends of Denmark.* Translated from the Danish and revised in collaboration with the author by L.M.Hollander (New York, 1919).

Chambers, R. W., 'Beowulf and the Heroic Age,' foreword to Archibald Strong's verse translation of *Beowulf* (London, 1925). Reprinted in *Man's Unconquerable Mind,* pp.53–69 (London, 1939).

Chambers, R. W., *England before the Norman Conquest* (London, 1926). Excerpts from source-material.

Routh, H. V., *God, Man, and Epic Poetry*, 2 vols. (Cambridge, Eng., 1927). See especially ii, ch.2.

Hodgkin, R. H., *A History of the Anglo-Saxons*, 2 vols. (Oxford, 1935). To the death of Alfred. Full, readable, splendidly illustrated.

SPECIAL TOPICS

Anderson, L. F., *The Anglo-Saxon Scop*. University of Toronto Studies, Phil. Series 1 (Toronto, 1903).

Rickert, E., 'The Old English Offa-saga,' in *Mod. Phil.*, ii,29–76, 321–376 (1904–5).

Hanscom, E. D., 'The feeling for nature in Old English poetry,' in *Jour. Eng. and Germ. Phil.*, v,439–63 (1905).

Emerson, O. F., 'Legends of Cain, especially in Old and Middle English,' in *Publ. Mod. Lang. Assn.*, xxi,831–929 (1906).

Lawrence, W. W., 'Some disputed questions in Beowulf-criticism,' in *Publ. Mod. Lang. Assn.*, xxiv,220–73 (1909).

Rankin, J. W., 'A study of the kennings in Anglo-Saxon poetry,' in *Jour. Eng. and Germ. Phil.*, viii,357–422; ix,49–84 (1909–10).

Klaeber, Fr., 'Aeneis und Beowulf,' in *Archiv für das Studium der neueren Sprachen und Literaturen*, cxxvi,40–48,339–59 (1911).

Lawrence, W. W., 'The haunted mere in *Beowulf*,' in *Publ. Mod. Lang. Assn.*, xxvii,208–45 (1912).

Stjerna, K., *Essays on Questions Connected with the Old English Poem of Beowulf*, translated and edited by J.R.Clark Hall (Coventry, 1912).

Deutschbein, M., 'Beowulf der Gautenkönig,' in *Festschrift für Lorenz Morsbach*, pp.291–7 (Halle, 1913).

Lawrence, W. W., '*Beowulf* and the Tragedy of Finnsburg,' in *Publ. Mod. Lang. Assn.*, xxx,372–431 (1915).

Flom, G. T., 'Alliteration and variation in Old Germanic name giving,' in *Mod. Lang. Notes*, xxxii,7–17 (1917).

Lawrence, W. W., 'The dragon and his lair in *Beowulf*,' in *Publ. Mod. Lang. Assn.*, xxxiii,547–83 (1918).

Björkman, E., *Studien über die Eigennamen im Beowulf.* Morsbachs Studien, lviii (Halle, 1920).

Cook, A. S., 'The possible begetter of the Old English *Beowulf* and *Widsith,*' in *Trans. of the Conn. Acad. of Arts and Sciences,* xxv,281–346 (1922).

Williams, R. A., *The Finn Episode in Beowulf* (Cambridge, Eng., 1924).

Pons, E., *La Thème et le Sentiment de la Nature dans la Poésie anglo-saxonne.* Publications de l'Université de Strasbourg, Fasc.25 (Strasbourg and London, 1925).

Wyld, H. C., 'Diction and Imagery in Anglo-Saxon Poetry,' in *Essays and Studies by members of the English Association,* xi,49–91 (1925).

Chambers, R.W., 'The Lost Literature of Medieval England,' in *The Library,* 4th series, v,293–321 (1925).

Malone, K., 'Hrethric,' in *Publ. Mod. Lang. Assn.,* xlii,268–313 (1927).

Phillpotts, B. S., 'Wyrd and Providence in Anglo-Saxon Thought,' in *Essays and Studies by members of the English Association,* xiii,7–27 (1928).

Lawrence, W. W., '*Beowulf* and the *Saga of Samson the Fair,*' in *Studies in English Philology, A Miscellany in honor of Frederick Klaeber* (Minneapolis, 1929).

Schücking, L., 'Das Königsideal im *Beowulf,*' in *Bulletin of the Mod. Hum. Res. Assn.,* iii,143–54 (1929). Also in *Englische Studien,* lxvii,1–14 (1932).

Andrew, S. O., *The Old English Alliterative Measure* (Croydon, 1931).

Haber, T. B., *A Comparative Study of the Beowulf and the Aeneid* (Princeton, 1931).

DuBois, A. E., 'The Unity of *Beowulf,*' in *Publ. Mod. Lang. Assn.,* xlix,374–405 (1934).

Girvan, R., *Beowulf and the Seventh Century* (London, 1935).

Kennedy, C. W., *Old English Elegies, translated into alliterative verse, with a critical introduction* (Princeton, 1936).

Sedgefield, W. J., 'The Scenery in *Beowulf*,' in *Jour. Eng. and Germ. Phil.*, xxxv,161–9 (1936).

Tolkien, J. R. R., 'Beowulf: The Monsters and the Critics,' *Proceedings of the British Academy*, xxii,245–95 (London, 1936).

Malone,K.,'Swerting,' in *The Germanic Review*,xiv,235–57 (1939).

Pope, J. C., *The Rhythm of Beowulf* (New Haven, 1942).

A GLOSSARY OF PROPER NAMES

A GLOSSARY OF PROPER NAMES

(Spellings in parentheses indicate approximate pronunciations)

ÆLFHERE (Alf' herra), a kinsman of Wiglaf.

ÆSCHERE (Ash'herra), a Dane; Hrothgar's beloved councillor and companion-in-arms; killed and carried off by Grendel's mother.

BEANSTAN (Bay'an stan), a Bronding, father of Breca.

BEOWULF (Bay'o wolf), not the hero of the poem; a Danish king mentioned in lines 18 and 53 as an ancestor of Hrothgar.

BEOWULF (Bay'o wolf), the hero of the poem; prince, and later king, of the Geats; son of Ecgtheow; on his mother's side grandson of Hrethel and nephew of Hygelac; slayer of the monsters and the dragon.

BRECA (Brekka), a prince of the Brondings; mentioned by Unferth as having defeated Beowulf in a youthful swimming match.

BRONDINGS, a tribe ruled by Breca.

BROSINGS, owners of a precious necklace which was possibly the same as the Brising necklace of the Elder Edda; the necklace presented to Beowulf after his defeat of Grendel is compared to the Brosings' necklace.

CAIN, the Biblical slayer of his brother Abel. In two passages in the poem (104–14; 1260–66) Grendel and his mother are represented as belonging to the brood of monsters which, according to medieval legend, were descended from Cain.

DÆGHREFN (Dag'raven), a warrior of the Hugas; killed in battle by Beowulf at the time of Hygelac's expedition against the Franks.

DANES, also referred to in the poem as North-, South-, East-, and West-Danes, and as Bright-Danes, Spear-Danes, Ring-Danes; known also as Ingwines (friends of Ing) and Scyldings (descendants of Scyld). At the time of the action of the poem the ruler of the Danes was Hrothgar.

EADGILS (Ay'ad gils), a Swedish prince; son of Ohthere;

grandson of Ongentheow. With his brother Eanmund, Eadgils rebelled against the rule of their uncle, Onela, and fled for protection to the Geats over whom Heardred, son of Hygelac, was ruling. Onela in revenge attacked the Geats, slew Eanmund and Heardred, and left Beowulf to rule. Subsequently Beowulf aided Eadgils in war against Onela.

EANMUND (Ay'an mund), a Swedish prince; brother of Eadgils.

ECGLAF (Edge'laf), a Dane; father of Unferth.

ECGTHEOW (Edge'thay o), father of Beowulf; husband of King Hrethel's only daughter.

ECGWELA (Edge'wella), an ancient Danish king.

EOFOR (Ay'o vor), a Geatish warrior who rescued his brother Wulf and slew the Swedish king, Ongentheow, in the battle of Ravenswood.

EOMÆR (Ay'o mare), son of King Offa of the Angles.

EORMANRIC (Ay'or man ric), king of the East Goths.

EOTAN, Jutes, who at Finnsburg fought under Finn against the Danes.

FINN, a Frisian king; husband of Hildeburh, a Danish princess; slain at Finnsburg by the Danes.

FINNS, a tribe, probably of Northern Norway, on whose shores Beowulf landed after his swimming match with Breca.

FINNSBURG, the stronghold of the Frisian king, Finn.

FITELA (Fit'el a), nephew and son of Sigemund whose slaying of the dragon is told by the minstrel in Heorot; in the Norse *Volsungasaga* known as Sinfjötli, son of Sigemund and his sister, Signy.

FOLCWALDA (Folk'wal da), father of the Frisian king, Finn.

FRANKS, the continental tribe attacked by Hygelac in the famous raid in which he met his death, and in which Beowulf slew Dæghrefn and escaped by swimming back to Sweden.

FREAWARU (Fray'a war uh), daughter of Hrothgar; betrothed to Ingeld as a 'peace-weaver' to end the feud between the Danes and the Heathobards. Beowulf prophesies to Hygelac that the feud will be renewed in spite of the marriage.

FRIESLAND, home of the Frisians.

FRISIANS, a tribe ruled by Finn; also mentioned (1207) as allied with the Franks against Hygelac.

FRODA, king of the Heathobards; father of Ingeld.

GARMUND, father of King Offa of the Angles.

GEATS (Gay'ats), a tribe located in South Sweden; also referred to in the poem as War-, Sea-, and Weder-Geats, and as Weders and Hrethlings (descendants of Hrethel). At the time of Beowulf's fight against the monsters the Geats were ruled by Hygelac. He was succeeded by his son, Heardred. After Heardred's death, Beowulf ruled for fifty years, and died of wounds received in the dragon fight.

GIFTHS, an East Germanic tribe.

GRENDEL, a monster, of human form but more than human size and strength; with his hag-like mother, had his lair in an evil pool near Heorot. Their raids on the hall took such toll of Hrothgar's warriors that for twelve years the hall was unused and deserted. Beowulf's struggle against these monsters occupies the first two-thirds of the poem.

GUTHLAF (Gooth'laf), a Danish warrior who fought at Finnsburg.

HÆRETH (Har'eth), father of Hygelac's wife, Hygd.

HÆTHCYN (Hath'kin), prince of the Geats; son of Hrethel. He (inadvertently) killed his brother Herebeald, ruled for a time, and was slain by the Swedish king Ongentheow at Ravenswood.

HALF-DANES, a people mentioned in the *Finnsburg Lay* to whom belong Hoc, Hnæf, and Hildeburh.

HALGA, a Danish prince; brother of Hrothgar; father of Hrothulf.

HAMA, a figure of Gothic legend who stole the Brosing necklace.

HEALFDENE (Hay'alf den na), a Danish king; father of Hrothgar, Heorogar, Halga, and an unnamed daughter.

HEARDRED (Hay'ard red), son of Hygelac; after Hygelac's death, king of the Geats; slain by the Swedish king Onela; succeeded by Beowulf.

HEATHOBARDS (Hay'a tho bards'), a Germanic tribe to which belonged King Froda, and his son Ingeld. Hrothgar attempted to end the feud between the Danes and the Heathobards by the marriage of his daughter Freawaru to Ingeld.

HEATHOLAF (Hay'a tho laf), a member of the Wylfing tribe; killed by Ecgtheow, father of Beowulf, who then fled to the young King Hrothgar for protection.

HEATHO-RÆMAS (Hay'a tho ray'mas), a tribe of Southern Norway on whose shores Breca was cast up after his swimming match with Beowulf.

HELMINGS, the people of Wealhtheow, wife of Hrothgar.

HEMMING, kinsman of Offa and Eomær, of the Angles.

HENGEST, leader of the Danes at Finnsburg after the death of Hnæf.

HEOROGAR (Hay'o ro gar), a brother of Hrothgar, and father of Heoroweard.

HEOROT (Hay'o rot), the famous hall of the Danes built by Hrothgar and haunted for twelve years by Grendel and his mother. The site of Heorot is usually located near the modern village of Leire in the island of Seeland.

HEOROWEARD (Hay'o ro way ard), son of Heorogar, and nephew of Hrothgar; slain by a follower of the dead Hrothulf at the fall of Heorot.

HEREBEALD (Her'ra bay old), eldest son of King Hrethel of the Geats; killed (inadvertently) by his brother, Hæthcyn.

HEREMOD (Her'ra mod), an ancient Danish king twice mentioned in the poem as an example of cruelty and avarice.

HERERIC (Her'ra ric), brother of Hygelac's wife, Hygd, and uncle of Heardred.

HETWARE (Het'war eh), a Frankish tribe against whom Hygelac fought in his last raid.

HILDEBURH, a Danish princess, and wife of the Frisian king, Finn.

HNÆF (Hnaf), brother of Hildeburh; leader of the Danes at Finnsburg; slain in the battle.

HOC, father of Hildeburh and Hnæf.

HONDSCIO (Hond'she o), a Geat; one of the band of four-teen warriors who accompanied Beowulf to Heorot; killed and devoured by Grendel.

HREOSNABEORH (Hray' os na bay'orh), a hill in Geat-land; scene of an attack on the Geats by Ohthere and Onela.

HRETHEL, king of the Geats; father of Hygelac, and grand-father of Beowulf.

HRETHLINGS, descendants of Hrethel; Geats.

HRETHMEN, Geats.

HRETHRIC, a son of Hrothgar.

HRONESNÆSS, a headland on the coast of Geatland on which Beowulf's burial barrow was built.

HROTHGAR, son of Healfdene; brother of Heorogar and Halga; father of Hrethric, Hrothmund and Freawaru; king of the Danes at the time of Beowulf's fight against the monsters; builder of Heorot.

HROTHMUND, a son of Hrothgar.

HROTHULF, son of Halga and nephew of Hrothgar. Pas-sages in the poem foreshadow the treachery of Hrothulf, after Hrothgar's death, in killing Hrethric and seizing the rule, only to be attacked in turn, and killed, by his cousin, Heoroweard.

HRUNTING, the name of the sword lent to Beowulf by Unferth, and used by Beowulf against Grendel's mother.

HUGAS, a Frankish tribe.

HUNLAFING, a son of Hunlaf, a warrior who fought under Hengest at Finnsburg.

HYGD, daughter of Hæreth, and wife and queen of Hygelac.

HYGELAC, son of Hrethel; uncle of Beowulf; ruler of the Geats.

INGELD, a prince of the Heathobards; son of Froda; betrothed to Hrothgar's daughter Freawaru.

INGWINE (Ing'winna), Ing's friends; Danes.

NÆGLING (Nag'ling), the name of the sword used by Beowulf against the dragon.

OFFA, king of the Continental tribe of Angles.

OHTHERE (Oht'herra), a Swedish prince; son of King Ongentheow; brother of Onela; father of Eanmund and Eadgils.

ONELA, a Swedish king; brother of Ohthere.

ONGENTHEOW (On'gen thay o), a Swedish king; father of Ohthere and Onela.

OSLAF, a Danish warrior who fought at Finnsburg.

RAVENSWOOD, a forest in Sweden; site of the battle between the Swedes and Geats in which Hygelac overthrew Ongentheow.

SCYLD (Shild), mythical founder of the Danish royal line.

SCYLDINGS (Shildings), descendants of Scyld; Danes.

SCYLFINGS (Shilfings), Swedes.

SIGEMUND, uncle and father of Fitela (Sinfjötli); Sigemund, the Volsung.

SWERTING, uncle, or grandfather, of Hygelac.

THRYTH, the shrewish wife of King Offa of the Angles. In the poem a contrast is drawn between Thryth and the gracious young Hygd, Hygelac's queen.

UNFERTH, the *thyle*, or spokesman, of Hrothgar, who taunted Beowulf with having been defeated by Breca in a youthful swimming match.

WÆGMUNDINGS (Wag'mundings), the family to which belonged Weohstan, Wiglaf, and Beowulf.

WÆLS, father of Sigemund.

WÆLSING, son of Wæls, Sigemund.

WAYLAND, the famous smith of Germanic legend.

WEALHTHEOW (Way'alh thay o), wife and queen of Hrothgar; mother of Hrethric and Hrothmund.

WENDELS, the tribe to which Wulfgar belonged; an uncertain tribe, possibly inhabitants of Vendel in Sweden or of Vendill in North Jutland.

WEOHSTAN (Way'oh stan), a Wægmunding; father of Wiglaf.

WIGLAF, a Wægmunding; kinsman of Beowulf, and his loyal companion-in-arms in the fatal battle against the dragon.

WITHERGYLD, a Heathobard warrior.

WONRED, a Geat; father of Wulf and Eofor.

WULF, a Geat; son of Wonred; fought in the battle of

Ravenswood; was wounded by Ongentheow, and rescued by his brother, Eofor.

WULFGAR, prince of the Wendels, and herald at Hrothgar's court.

WYLFINGS, a Germanic tribe to which belonged the Heatholaf who was killed by Ecgtheow, Beowulf's father.

WYRD, Fate.

YRMENLAF, a Dane; younger brother of Æschere, the friend and councillor of Hrothgar who was killed and carried off by Grendel's mother.